MODERN RUNES

MODERN RUNES

Discover the Magic of Casting and
Divination for Everyday Life

Vervain Helsdottir

ROCKRIDGE
PRESS

For general information on our other products and services or to obtain technical support, please contact our Customer Care Department within the United States at (866) 744-2665, or outside the United States at (510) 253-0500.

Rockridge Press publishes its books in a variety of electronic and print formats. Some content that appears in print may not be available in electronic books, and vice versa.

Interior and Cover Designer: John Clifford
Art Producer: Tom Hood
Editor: Sean Newcott
Production Manager: Holly Haydash
Production Editor: Melissa Edeburn

Illustrations © Tartila, 2020.
Author photo courtesy of Shawn Johnson.

ISBN: Print 978-1-64739-020-4 | eBook 978-1-64739-021-1
R0

gefinn Óðni
sjálfr sjálfum mér

CONTENTS

PART
TWO

READING RUNES TODAY   57

INTRODUCTION

In the modern world, it can be all too easy to feel complete separation from our natural environment. The more removed we are, the less we understand our inner natures. The runes offer an antidote to this separation by connecting us to the fundamental mysteries of human life as preserved in the symbol language of the ancient northern Europeans. These symbols hold potent meaning that is just as applicable today as it was 2,000 years ago. Ragnarök may be the end of one world, but it is also the beginning of a new one. Whenever the world threatens to fall apart, my fellow rune-workers and I have turned to the runes for wisdom in the darkness and have received insights about how to light the way forward. I hope you will find them similarly enriching.

My initiation into the runes has been a long, slow process. I began keeping my private journals in runes when I was 11 years old, but it was not easy for sheltered preteens to access esoteric runelore in 2004. I didn't seriously engage with runes until I began working with Óðinn nine years later, at which point they began to speak to me. When I invoked them, my world changed, my life changed, I changed. I read more about them, found fellow rune-seekers, and continued to practice and reflect. Three years ago, I was called to invite the runes into my body, and I experienced a series of further runic initiations in which each rune showed itself to me clearly in my lived reality. These initiations, along with my years of research, study, and experimentation, have informed the much-distilled contents of this book.

It's challenging to present the runes in a way that is simultaneously approachable, actionable, and accurate because runelore is complex. You can read many books about the runes and find different (and sometimes conflicting) information in all of them. The most accurate sources are the old rune poems, but they are both enigmatic and incomplete. Much is left to discover.

This book is not intended to provide a complete survey of runelore and rune magic or plumb the depths of the runic mysteries. You must access these mysteries within yourself, and you can understand them only through direct experience. No book or teacher can replace long-term study and meditation or the less voluntary experience of runic initiation, but neither can intuition and experimentation replace research. This book shares the essence of various interpretations of historic and esoteric runelore, along with my own thoughts and suggestions for your study and practice of the runes. I hope this book will serve as a foundation for further exploration of this magical symbol language and its meaning in the modern age.

Think of this book as an introductory language textbook that will help you recognize the runes when they are calling, comprehend their meaning when they speak, and say what you mean when you invoke them. Merely reading the book will not make you fluent, but engaging more deeply with the material and dedicating yourself to your practice will. Fluency with the futhark grants access to greater understanding of our lived everyday reality. When you employ this knowledge properly, you will be able to interpret the unseen and rewrite your destiny. This path makes great demands of you, but the rewards are beyond imagination. If the path does not call you, that's okay. If it does, seek the mysteries—or, as it is often said in Old Norse, *reyn til runa*!

ONE

THE REALM OF RUNES

We live in a wondrous world filled with beauty and challenges.
The runes, a set of mysterious symbols developed by an ancient people,
describe the most fundamental facets of that world and the glorious act
of living in it. This world *is* the magical world, and the runes are accessible
to us today through study, meditation, and practice. Once you are
familiar with their shapes and meanings, you will begin to see their
magic everywhere.

The first half of this book helps you contextualize the runes in the
world of their origin and in the modern world. The magic of the runes is
as relevant today as ever, but much of the available scholarship on the
subject is devoted to interpreting the runes as they would have been
understood nearly 2,000 years ago. The historical background is
important for rooting your understanding of the runes in their original
context and serves as a foundation for the modern interpretations and
applications in the second half of the book. Are you ready? Come with
me to the world tree Yggdrasil and let us look together upon the Web of
Wyrd, the original home of the runes.

CHAPTER

1

A MYSTICAL BUT MODERN MEANS OF DIVINATION

It was almost two millennia ago when Óðinn, king of Ásgarðr and Norse god of magic, wisdom, ecstasy, inspiration, war, and death, reached down from the branches of the world tree Yggdrasil and took up the runes and their secrets from within the Well of Urðr. Although the runes and their use in magic are ancient, the history of their use in divination is uncertain. There are only vague references to the casting and reading of runes, and modern rune magicians must derive a cohesive working system from an amalgam of historical research, intuition, discourse, and experience. We may never know their full past, but the runes are very much alive in the present, and they will share their secrets. All you have to do is ask.

THE SACRED ALPHABET

The word *runes* is an umbrella term used to refer to several ancient and medieval writing systems used for transcribing early Germanic languages. They may be derived from Latin, but scholars do not agree on the source of inspiration.

Runes were in use from at least the second century CE, and their use spread throughout northern Europe, Britain, Scandinavia, and Iceland until their decline toward the end of the medieval era. The earliest confirmed runic inscriptions date from around 150 CE and are written in Elder Futhark runes, which were in use until about 800 CE. Early inscriptions were exclusive to the upper classes until the beginning of the Viking Age, around 700 CE. Over time, the Elder Futhark evolved into many futharks: the Anglo-Saxon Futhorc (circa 400–1100 CE), the Younger Futhark (circa 800–1100 CE), Medieval runes (circa 1100–1500 CE), and Dalecarlian runes, which were in use in the Swedish province of Dalarna from about 1500 CE into the 20th century. Among these, the best known today is the Elder Futhark.

Across all runic systems, each rune is made up almost exclusively of vertical and diagonal lines, with very few horizontal or curved elements. The runes likely employ an angular design because they were primarily carved into wood and stone. It is much easier to produce straight lines in both materials, and it is easier to carve with the grain of wood than against it, which probably accounts for the absence of horizontal lines. Runic inscriptions were written from left to right and right to left, sometimes with multiple lines reading in opposite directions. The direction of text seemingly has no significance, but the runes themselves typically face the same direction as the flow of text; that is, lines written right to left typically use mirrored versions of the runes.

From the start, the runes were seen as sacred and magical. After all, the power of writing is the seemingly magical ability to communicate ideas across time and space. Magic was a natural part of everyday life for the ancients, and the vocabulary of meanings assigned to the runes likely preexisted the letters themselves. If you dig deeper, you will find that the modern definition of a rune as a letter of sorts is only the most superficial. Although the etymology of the word is uncertain, *rune* has cognates meaning "secret," "mystery," "whisper," "roar," "wisdom," and "counsel," as well as "letter." Spells and prayers were written in runes on amulets and weapons, and sometimes individual runes, or *bindrunes*, were written on these items as initials, abbreviations, or magical symbols.

The Elder Futhark

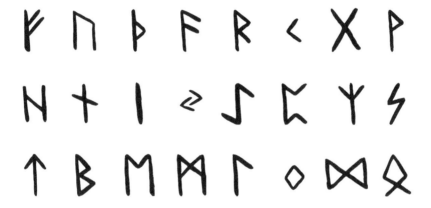

The Elder Futhark is the oldest futhark and was used from approximately 150 to 800 CE. The oldest confirmed runic inscription (circa 150 CE) is carved into an antler comb and reads ᚺᚨᚱᛊᚨ (*Harja*, meaning "warrior").

Elder Futhark comprises 24 runes organized into three rows of eight, known as *ættir* (singular *ætt*, meaning "eight"). Just as the word *alphabet* is derived from the Greek *alpha* and *beta*, *futhark* comes from the first six runes of the first ætt (ᚠᚢᚦᚨᚱᚲ), which spell *futhark*. The earliest known sequential listing of the Elder Futhark is found on the Kylver Stone, circa 400 CE.

Modern rune magicians (myself included) most frequently use the Elder Futhark. No one has discovered a rune poem for the Elder Futhark, however, so some of our best clues about the meanings of the runes come from the poems about the Younger Futhark and Anglo-Saxon rune row.

The Younger Futhark

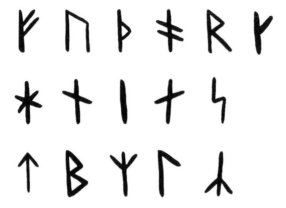

The Younger Futhark came into use in the ninth century CE as Proto-Norse evolved into Old Norse. Edred Thorsson posits that the Younger Futhark was developed primarily for magico-religious reasons, noting that the rune row was culled and simplified as the sound system of the language became more complex. Regardless of the intent, the rune row is lacking for the needs of a modern runecaster. The Elder runes that are missing from the Younger Futhark are some of the most magically potent, and the symbol language feels incomplete without them.

Whereas the use of the Elder Futhark was limited to the educated elite, the Younger Futhark became commonplace, and people used it quite casually, often to carve ancient graffiti, such as "Tholfir Kolbeinsson carved these runes high up."

The Younger Futhark has several variants, including Long Branch Runes (typically considered the standard forms), Short Twig Runes (a mix of standard and simplified forms), and Staveless Runes (featuring minimalist versions of all 16 Younger runes). The Norwegian and Icelandic Rune Poems, as well as the *Abecedarium Nordmannicum,* describe the Younger Futhark.

The Anglo-Saxon Futhorc

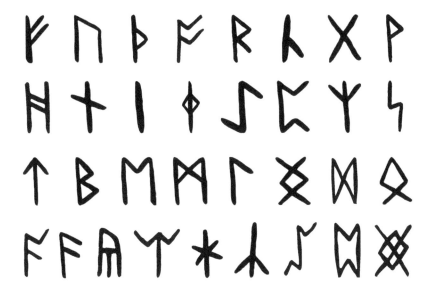

The Anglo-Saxon Futhorc first appeared in the 5th century CE and was in use through the 11th century CE. The Futhorc did not develop all at once and was adapted throughout the duration of its use, so there is no "one true Anglo-Saxon Futhorc." Changes and additions were made slowly, and in its earliest inscriptions, the Futhorc is nearly impossible to differentiate from the Elder Futhark. The only known complete inscription of a version of the Anglo-Saxon rune row is found on the Seax of Beagnoth, a blade presumed to have been enchanted for use in battle.

ÓÐINN AND THE DISCOVERY OF THE RUNES

Although the material origin of the runes is unclear, the *Hávamál* ("The Words of the High One") relates the mythical tale of their discovery by Óðinn, the Norse god of magic, wisdom, ecstasy, inspiration, war, and death.

At the center of all things, guarded and tended by the Norns, Yggdrasil, the world tree, grows. At its feet is the Well of Urðr (*Urðarbrunnr*, the "well of fate," "well of wyrd"), the primordial home of the runes. In his quest for wisdom and knowledge, Óðinn journeyed to the tree above the well and hung himself upon its branches. For nine days and nine nights, he hung from Yggdrasil, wounded by his own spear, Gungnir. He had no respite from hunger, thirst, or pain. Historically, death by spear was the preferred method of sacrificing animals or enemies to Óðinn, so this was a sacrifice of Óðinn's uninitiated self to Óðinn's higher self (*gefinn Oðni*, "given to Óðinn"). As a god, he could not truly die (that is, stop existing) on that tree. Only his uninitiated ego would die and be reborn initiated into the mysteries and magic of the runes.

In his fasting-induced ecstasy, Óðinn received a vision of the threads of the universe and the ways in which they are woven together. He understood the patterns, the relationships—the runes. Inspired, renewed, and filled with wisdom, he cried out as he took them up from the well, then fell back from the branches of Yggdrasil to the earth. From there he went forth, made rich and fertile with the wisdom and knowledge of the runic mysteries, and began to share this knowledge with others. Over millennia, this knowledge has been passed down from runemaster to apprentice for generations. Now, through this book, it begins to find its way to you.

CHAPTER

2

RUNES IN PRESENT-DAY PRACTICE

Ancient as they are, the runes are very much alive and powerful today. We cannot directly access the past, but we can participate in the present and cocreate the future. With the help of the runes, we can learn to better understand our past and present, as well as the forces that shape our future. As we come to deeper understandings through observation, divination, practice, and experimentation, the magic of the runes can help us become our highest selves for the highest good of all.

RUNESTONES: THEN AND NOW

Historically, runestones were ancient standing stones carved with runic inscriptions, often marking special burial sites. While most of these inscriptions merely contain the names of the dead and perhaps what they did, magical inscriptions have been found on standing stones, weapons, and jewelry.

To the ancient Norse, runes were a writing system as well as a system of magic. Each rune contained not only a sound but also a secret. Ancient Norse used runes to write prayers and spells, record business transactions, note the names of the dead, and record the carvers' names.

Despite the evidence for the runes' magical significance, little information is available about their ancient use in divination. The Roman historian Tacitus's first-century work *Germania* notes that lots for divination were cut from a tree and marked with various symbols before being cast and interpreted, and runes were also likely used in this way. The *Rúnatáls-Þáttr-Óðins* (verses 143–145) supports this belief. If wooden pieces had been carved with runes and cast for insight, it is unlikely that any would have survived because wood is perishable. In any case, the lack of a clear historical precedent for runic divination does not mean we cannot do it today. Magic has always been a living art.

Just as tarot cards can be used in spellwork to empower the forces corresponding to their divinatory meanings, you can interpret the runes in a divinatory context according to their magical meanings and purposes. Modern rune readers select individual runes from a bag or casting cloth before interpreting them according to their individual meanings and juxtapositions. Today, runestones are usually sets of pebble-like stones, disks, or tiles carved with individual runes and used for divination. You can purchase a set at metaphysical bookstores and in many crystal shops, and they are widely available online, although many practitioners choose to make their own.

REVIVING RUNES FOR THE MODERN WORLD

The runic revival can be traced back to Johannes Bureus, who lived in the late 16th and early 17th centuries. After learning of Dalecarlian runes, Bureus developed his own system, which he called *Adalruna*. The Adalrunes contained elements of Norse runes and runelore but were influenced by Judeo-Christian mysticism. In the 19th century, Guido von List turned his attention to the runes after experiencing a runic initiation during extended post-surgery blindness. He devised a system based on his vision called the Armanen runes, which corresponded to the 18 runes described in the *Rúnatáls-Þáttr-Óðins*, and later founded Wotanism. Unfortunately, his work was polluted by his racist agenda, which continues to taint segments of modern Heathenry and runework today.

Siegfried Adolf Kummer continued this misuse of the runes, as did high-ranking Nazi Party members Heinrich Himmler and Karl Maria Wiligut. Himmler was interested in using Nordic mysticism to prove the superiority of the Germanic peoples, and Wiligut served as a runic consultant and occult adviser. The Schutzstaffel insignia ᛋᛋ was made up of two Sol/Sig runes, and the swastika was the ancient solar wheel. Whether the inherent powers of the runes were at work in the rise and fall of the Third Reich is open for debate, but they were certainly invoked.

The 20th-century runic revival was rescued by Karl Spiesberger. In his book *Runenmagie*, he reformed the Armanen system and synthesized the work of earlier rune revivalists while removing the racist elements. The Elder Futhark was not revived for contemporary use until Edred Thorsson published *Futhark: A Handbook of Rune Magic* in 1979. *Futhark* is a foundational text for anyone seriously interested in exploring runelore and rune magic, but the work that has introduced most people to the runes over the past 40 years is Ralph Blum's well-intentioned but ahistorical *The Book of Runes*. This book uses the Elder Futhark runes (reordered with the addition of a blank rune) as an oracle, but is largely informed by the *I Ching*, an ancient Chinese divination text, and has very little to do with traditional runelore. Although Blum is straightforward about his sources and many people enjoy his writings and methods, his work is generally considered inaccurate. Fortunately, the tradition awakened by Thorsson has been continued by Freya Aswynn, Diana Paxson, and others (see Resources, page 126).

SEEKING GUIDANCE

The point of divination is not to relinquish responsibility but to gain wisdom and perspective that will empower you to make more informed decisions for yourself. Allegorically, we chart the stars so we can make better choices about where to steer our ship, not so we can blame the stars later when we end up lost in the middle of the ocean.

How does divination work? What are its limits? There are two core theories. The first holds that when working with a set of potent and complex symbols, any randomly selected symbol is liable to offer a beneficial lens through which to gain a new perspective on the situation at hand. Through deep consideration, reflection, and questioning, you can arrive at helpful new conclusions about your life path and how you might want to direct yourself forward into the future. In other words, every rune (or tarot card or tea leaf) has something to teach in every situation, and it is up to you to make the connections through reflective contemplation.

The second theory is more magical. We certainly project our experience into the symbols we see and weave narratives from the combinations of images and ideas that surface. But more often than not, the symbols that appear are *so* perfectly relevant to the current situation that they seem to be presented on purpose. You do not have to believe in a divine hand or cosmic consciousness to believe we can derive beneficial narratives from nearly any set of symbols, but *in my experience,* the rate of poignant coincidence is too high to ignore.

Building on this idea, the universe appears to speak to us in the way we are most open to receiving its guidance and most likely to understand the message. For some people, this message is delivered in books or through the words of strangers or friends. For others, the presence of certain plants, animals, or objects seems meaningful, and still others derive omens from seemingly random texts and emails. Those who seek a direct conversation with the universe may turn to prayer or divination. Runes may appear in the shapes of trees, fallen branches, or cracks in the sidewalk, or they may be consciously invited in the context of a runecasting (more on this in chapter 4).

It is easy to miss or misunderstand the signs you are sent, but through practice and honest reflection, you can cultivate an awareness of your blind spots and cognitive biases. It's helpful to keep a journal while you are developing your divinatory practice so you can record your readings and explore how relevant situations unfold. Recording your observations and reflections will help you recognize patterns in your thoughts, choices, and perceptions and better understand the runes in the context of your own life.

GAINING WISDOM

The runes typically represent relationships, characteristics, forces, and patterns of energy, rather than people and things, so be sure to formulate your questions so these sorts of answers will be valuable to you. You are unlikely to get a beneficial response to a yes-or-no question. Fortune-telling questions may be helpful in certain situations, but the future is not set in stone. Your choices can affect what unfolds, so you may not want to take the answers too seriously. Keep in mind that you are seeking information and perspective so *you* can make decisions. You are not looking for the runes to make decisions for you.

For example, you may be tempted to ask if you should break up with a partner. This question gives the runes little room to answer effectively and is also an abdication of your responsibility. Rework the question to ask what blessings and challenges the relationship provides, or inquire about the dominant energies of your partner, yourself, and the relationship as a whole. Open-ended questions give the runes the opportunity to provide you with information according to their native vocabulary. These kinds of questions help the runes flesh out your understanding so you can make more informed and nuanced decisions.

Questions starting with "What is the nature of," "What is the relationship between," "What energy can I call upon to achieve," "What blessings/challenges are provided by," or "How can I engage productively with" are ideal for inviting the runes to whisper helpful wisdom on any given topic. You can pose these and other open-ended questions on an infinite array of topics, such as career and lifestyle changes; relationships with coworkers, friends, and family; time and resource management; travel; global politics; health and personal development; and spirituality, spellwork, and creative projects. With permission, you can apply these same methods to readings for others. You'll find sample questions and readings in chapter 5.

EMBRACING THE JOURNEY

If you want easy answers and quick solutions, you won't find them here—or anywhere. If you choose to pursue the path of the runes, you will find they have much to teach at every turn. Although every new secret you unearth will reveal a greater portion of the unknown, the wisdom you gain will aid and empower you all your life. Runework is not the solution to all your troubles, and it will not eliminate effort and experimentation on your journey, but it is another helpful tool for meeting life's challenges. Learning to read runes will not lead you to winning lottery numbers or make your dilemmas disappear, but it can add new layers of meaning to your life and provide fresh perspectives and approaches for greater success. The only magic we can truly perform is transforming ourselves, and self-discovery can enable us to effect change on the world.

We need reminders to slow down and take in the world around us. We crave connection to the earth and to our ancestors and their ancient ways. Although the world has become more technologically advanced, humans have a diminished understanding of life's greatest mysteries.

The runes offer space for contemplation, perspective for reflection, and connection to the ancient past. As the fundamental units of sacred expression by an ancient people who lived completely and inseparably intertwined with Earth's natural cycles and who depended absolutely on Earth's grace, the runes offer a connection to deep and ancient mysteries. By listening to the runes' whispers, you are participating in an age-old tradition and choosing to see beyond the veil of noise inherent in modern living. The more we harness the power of modern technology according to the wisdom of our ancient ancestors, the closer we get to living in harmony with ourselves, our environment, and each other.

RUNES ARE ALL AROUND

Chances are, somewhere in your line of sight is a piece of technology bearing a bindrune. The Bluetooth logo is a bindrune of Younger Futhark runes Bjarkan and Hagall (ᛒ + ᚼ). Bluetooth technology is actually named for Harald Bluetooth, a medieval Scandinavian king who was famous for uniting the tribes of Denmark and part of Norway in a common purpose, in much the same way that Bluetooth technology unites multiple devices. Hagall ᛝ and Bjarkan/Berkana ᛒ represent the sounds of H and B, so the logo comprises a personal bindrune of King Harald Bluetooth's initials.

You also may have seen J. R. R. Tolkien's adaptation of runes on Thrór's map in the opening pages of *The Hobbit*. Although not strictly a bindrune, because it's made of Latin letters, Tolkien's insignia (found across his work) is constructed as a bindrune of his initials, JRRT. Tolkien was a professor of Anglo-Saxon and English language and literature at Oxford University, and his academic work informed his fictional work.

Nordic folk bands such as Wardruna and Heilung use runes in their songs, on their album covers, and throughout their branding, and many metal bands use runes or rune-like fonts to underscore their image. Many modern neo-pagans wear rune jewelry or have rune tattoos. Unfortunately, white supremacists also repurpose these sacred symbols for nefarious purposes. There is a modern movement to reclaim these ancient symbols from those who would pervert them, and the rune-wise are encouraged to share their knowledge of the true meanings of these symbols.

CHAPTER

CHOOSING YOUR RUNE SET

This chapter covers the types of runes you can purchase or make yourself as well as considerations in selecting a set of runes. It describes everything you need to know to prepare your runes for their first reading (and you for yours), including cleansing, consecrating, and charging.

FINDING YOUR RUNE SET

You can find premade sets of runes in occult bookstores and new age shops, at pagan events and renaissance fairs, in many crystal shops, and online. Semiprecious runestones are popular, and wood is traditional, but rune sets can be made from clay, antler, bone, metal, glass, or just about anything else. I made my very first set of runes out of pink sea glass that I painted with red nail polish. There's no limit to the variety of rune sets you can create or find, and you can certainly have more than one. The only limit is your imagination (and perhaps your budget), although many people find they have a better bond with runes made from natural materials. When picking out or creating your runes, consider shape, size, and texture. How will they feel in your hands? Think about the durability and source of the material, the quality of craftsmanship, and who made them.

Above all, the runes you use should feel good to *you*. Many people prefer to buy runes in person so they can run a vibe check before committing, but if you need to purchase them online, ask the universe or your guides to lead you to the best set for you. If you ask in good faith and fully expect a response, you will know the rune set when you come across it. You may also prefer to make your own runes, which is covered in this chapter.

MAKING YOUR OWN RUNES

If you like your magical tools to be personal and unique, making your own runes is the obvious path. You can create them out of anything, but it's best if the material is natural and durable and has meaning for you. The traditional choice would be living wood from a fruit- or nut-bearing tree, but stones, acorns, certain shells, clay, metal, and leather are all fine choices. Use what calls to you.

When gathering materials from nature, ask permission of the appropriate land wights or plant spirits, and always leave a suitable eco-friendly offering, such as honey, mead or wine, a crystal, or sacred herbs. When seeking consent, you will have to rely on your intuition and signs in the environment around you for the answer. A gentle breeze, a pleasant birdcall, or the appearance of a gentle creature is a positive sign. A prick or sting is a negative sign.

Once you know what material you want to use, it is easy to find basic tutorials for shaping, carving, and coloring your runes (see Resources, page 126). You give the runes form by shaping and carving them, spirit by intoning them, and lifeblood by coloring them. Traditionally, runes are first carved and then stained or painted, but carving may not be appropriate for every medium.

The most traditional coloring agent is the blood of the rune reader, often invoked symbolically with red ochre. You could use actual blood (if and only if you are certain of a safe, sterile technique), but most modern practitioners do not. Red paint, permanent marker, paint pen, or nail polish will work on most surfaces. You can use any other color, but make sure it has potent meaning for you.

Whatever media and methods you choose, keep the following principles in mind when crafting your own runes:

- Work in a ritual environment. Light candles, burn incense, put on some music—whatever makes the process more magical for you.

- The more effort, time, labor, care, and attention you put into your runes, the better your bond with the runes will be.

- Work through the runes in futhark order during each step of the process.

- Make sure the pieces are roughly uniform in shape, size, appearance, and feel so you can select blindly.

- Intone the runes while you are making them by chanting their names and sounds into their forms. During each stage, whisper, speak, or sing the rune's name and sound while simultaneously focusing on the rune's meanings.

- Keep your perception open. The runes may reveal new sides of themselves during the creative process. Be open to this, as they are speaking to you. If you don't listen now, they may not bother to speak to you in the future.

- Plan to make mistakes. The runes teach *many* lessons. In other words, have extra materials on hand to redo any runes you're not happy with, or make peace with imperfection.

Once you have shaped, written, and colored your runes, you may want to seal them. A sealant or topcoat will protect your hard work to a certain extent, but some people believe that such physical barriers also create magical barriers. You can seal wood with beeswax, and most materials have corresponding sealants available at craft stores and online.

Cleansing, Consecrating, and Charging Your Runes

Once you've procured your runes, you will need to cleanse, consecrate, and charge them. This process will help you bond with the runes and initiate them into your practice. You may do this in any way you see fit, so feel free to make personal adjustments to the following instructions.

Conduct the work in a ritual setting (see chapter 4 for suggestions on creating sacred space). You will need your casting cloth, runes, pouch, something to cleanse your runes (such as a bowl of salt, a lit candle, or a smoking cauldron of herbs or incense), oil or water for anointing, crystals (optional), and a wand (also optional; pointing a finger with conviction works just as well).

Lay out your runes in order on your casting cloth (in a single row or circle or in three rows of eight), state your intentions, and call upon any spirits you wish to have present for this process.

CLEANSING YOUR RUNES

Begin by cleansing your runes of any disharmonious energies they may have acquired using one or more of the following methods:

- To cleanse with salt, pick up the first rune and place it in the bowl of salt. Visualize the salt soaking up the disharmonious energies, take up the rune, and say, *"By salt of earth and salt of sea, Fehu is purified in thee."* Repeat this, one by one, with the rest of the runes.

- To cleanse with fire, pass each rune briefly through a candle's flame, saying, *"Purified by sacred flame, only Uruz now remains."* Repeat this, one by one, with the rest of the runes.

- To cleanse with smoke, safely burn herbs or resin incense in a small cauldron or other fireproof container in a well-ventilated area. Pass each rune through the smoke and say, *"By sacred smoke and smoldering flame, only Thurisaz now remains."* Repeat this, one by one, with the rest of the runes.

- You can cleanse waterproof runes by rinsing them in fresh water or salt water, or by leaving them on a patch of earth overnight, preferably during a dark moon.

  Repeat the cleansing process whenever your runes start to get energetically sticky or foggy.

CONSECRATING YOUR RUNES

After cleansing, it's time to consecrate your runes.

- Start by anointing yourself on your third eye, throat, and heart with a few drops of sacred oil or water.

- Anoint each rune with a touch of the same. Intone the runes as you do this, and feel their presence strengthen and become clearer and brighter.

CHARGING YOUR RUNES

You can charge your runes as frequently as you'd like. You should certainly do so before your first reading, but you can also charge them whenever they need a little freshening up.

  To charge your runes:

- If you are working with crystals (optional), arrange them around your runes so they point inward.

- Ground yourself and take a few deep breaths.

- Use your wand or finger to point at each rune in turn and trace its shape, simultaneously intoning its name or sound while focusing on its meaning and mystery.

- Repeat this process until you can feel the magic emanating from your runes.

When your runes have finished charging, place them in their pouch (you may want to cleanse and consecrate the pouch, as well) until they are ready to be cast for the first time.

Discovering a Set's Personality

In ancient times, such as described in the account of Tacitus, it's possible that the runes would have been cut and carved for a single rite and then ritually destroyed, but most modern rune magicians prefer to have an ongoing relationship with one or more sets of runes. As you and your runes work together over time, you will grow closer and become more comfortable collaborating. You may find that different sets have distinct attitudes, and you might develop particular relationships with each. One might have a sense of humor, and another might speak in riddles; one may be comforting and another brutal, although both speak true. Some rune sets become old friends, and some will grow distant. Eventually, you and your runes will come to develop your own vernacular, and sometimes you may find you understand the runes without quite knowing *how* you understand them—but that's exactly as it should be.

RUNESCRIPTS AND BINDRUNES

Runescripts and bindrunes are types of runic formulas, or ways of combining multiple runes and invoking them to activate magical intentions. Bindrunes synthesize multiple rune forms into one complex symbol, whereas runescripts comprise multiple runes in a linear order according to the intended effect. A bindrune is ideal for imbuing an object or person with a particular energy or intention. For example, you might place a bindrune of Elhaz, Ehwaz, and Othala on your front door to protect your home and maintain harmony within. There is a famous bindrune of Gebo and Ansuz found upon a lance shaft in Denmark that is thought to indicate a sacrifice to Óðinn.

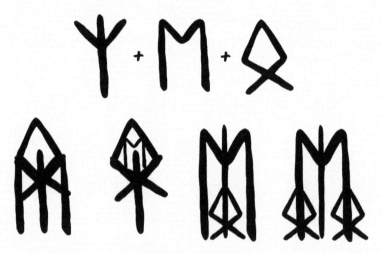

^ A bindrune of Elhaz, Ehwaz, and Othala

^ A famous bindrune of Gebo and Ansuz

^ A runescript of of Othala, Fehu, Jera, Wunjo, and Elhaz

Runescripts are more appropriate as part of spellwork to bring about a certain change or event. For example, you might create a runescript of Othala, Fehu, Jera, Wunjo, and Elhaz (in that order) to request that your wealth and property increase, that you reap the fruits of your labors, that this brings you joy, and that this abundance and joy is protected. A famous historical runescript is ALU (ᚨᛚᚢ), which you may want to chant aloud while staining, consecrating, or charging your runes, as it roughly represents the gift of life, consisting of breath and inspiration (Ansuz), lifeblood (Laguz), and physical form (Uruz). Formulate runescripts and bindrunes with care. You can inscribe them on paper, wood, living trees (with permission), stone, metal, fruit and other food items, magical tools and books, clothes, shoes, accessories, and nearly anything else. You can charge runescripts and bindrunes the same way you charge runes. Use a wand or finger to draw the shape of the runes while intoning their names and sounds and chanting ALU or the runescript itself.

Before you invoke a rune, be sure you have familiarized yourself with its full range of meanings through study and practice. If you don't know what it means before you invoke it, you sure will by the time it's done showing up.

^ The famous historical runescript ALU—Ansuz, Laguz, and Uruz

CHAPTER

4

HOW TO CAST RUNES

Finally, your runes are ready to emerge. Cleansed, consecrated, and charged, they are eagerly waiting to be plucked from their pouch and read for the first time. This chapter covers the essential materials for runecasting, along with the entire process from creating sacred space to closing your reading.

GATHER THE ESSENTIALS

As you read this section, keep in mind that all the bells and whistles of ritual are in service of creating the necessary *mind-set* for performing a rune reading or a work of magic. They can help, but a focused and dedicated practitioner does not have to rely on sensory aids. You need only approach the runes with faith, curiosity, and respect.

Although the runes will speak true as long as you appropriately invoke and respect them, taking the time to create a feeling of ritual and ceremony can open your mind to better receive their guidance. Use your own judgment to determine which of the following supplies you will purchase, repurpose, make, or do without:

- **Rune set.** At the bare minimum, you will need a set of runes to draw from and interpret. There's an app for that! Opinions vary regarding oracular apps, but there *are* options.

- **Bag or pouch.** You will need a bag or pouch to contain your runes when not in use and from which you will select runes for a reading. Boxes can work, but pouches are better at keeping secrets.

- **Rune meanings.** Eventually you'll carry these in your mind, but for now this book can serve as your reference.

- **Casting cloth.** It is polite and traditional to cast the runes upon a cloth rather than directly onto the table or the ground. A dedicated cloth is best, but a handkerchief or a paper dinner napkin is better than nothing. The cloth defines a magical boundary, helps keep the runes clean, and symbolizes the Well and Web of Wyrd.

- **Personal objects and talismans.** You may want to have other talismans, sacred objects, and personal belongings present for your reading, such as representations of your gods and guides, plant and crystal allies, or certain jewelry.

- **Journal and writing implement.** Reflecting upon your rune readings in your journal is part of the reading, not an extra step you do afterward.

Writing (and then going back and reading) a rune journal will help you process the thoughts, feelings, and ideas that come up during your readings, keep you accountable to yourself, and improve the quality of your readings over time.

Set Your Intentions

So much of what you get out of a reading hinges on how you set your intentions and formulate your questions before you call upon the wisdom of the runes. When you're fully attuned to your question and the nuances of the situation, you're better prepared to receive specific guidance and make relevant connections because you are more able to notice relevant details. You can use your rune journal *before* a reading to map out your situation and work out your questions as concisely as possible.

In Douglas Adams's *The Hitchhiker's Guide to the Galaxy*, a great fuss is made over discovering the answer to "life, the universe, and everything," which turns out to be "forty-two"—only no one knows what the *question* is. It is the same with runes. It doesn't help to know the answer is Gebo ᛉ if you aren't clear on the question. Take care to formulate your questions so there is little to no doubt as to what the answers mean. The better you get to know the runes and their natures, the better you will understand the sorts of questions they are best at answering.

Creating Sacred Space

A ritual environment is not necessary for the runes to work. It is for your benefit as their reader. The runes are ever-present and always whispering, but your mind is not always silent and ready to hear their wisdom. Conducting your readings in sacred space will help quiet your mind to hear the whispers, prepare your consciousness to make the necessary connections, and remind you that divination is not a tool to be used on a whim. You must incorporate the wisdom you glean into the actions of your daily life, and that takes time and effort. If you are unwilling to dedicate time and effort to your reading, how can you commit to elevating yourself to the level of the wisdom you receive?

Make sure you will not be disturbed or distracted during the reading, and give yourself plenty of time. The space can be indoors or outdoors, but it should be free of clutter, and you should be able to hear your own thoughts. Consider including music, incense, candles, essential oils, crystals, and plants in your rune rituals and readings.

It is best to use the same space and basic elements for most of your runework. If you do it in the same setting every time, context-dependent memory will make it easier for you to slip into an oracular or magical mind-set. You can, however, change certain details to fit your reading. Light particular candles or bring different crystals or talismans to the reading, depending on the topic. Experiment as spirit calls you, and over time you will find balance between ritual repetition and situational tailoring.

PREPARE FOR A CASTING

Before you get settled into your space, make sure you have everything you need. Candles? Lighter? Jacket, shawl, or blanket? Pen? Moisturize, hydrate, and relieve yourself *before* you begin the ritual so you're not going in and out of sacred space during the reading or distracted by your own discomfort. Dress for the occasion. Put on a rose quartz necklace or your favorite lipstick before you look into your love life, or pour yourself (and any spirits present) a glass of the good stuff before you and the runes start talking money. You may also want to cast a circle around your rune-space.

A traditional setup includes an altar placed physically below the seated reader, such as a low table, but there are lots of options, so make yourself comfortable. Make sure you have ample space and a place to journal while the runes are still out. Lay out your casting cloth, and arrange your talismans, journal, and anything else you require according to your intuition. Place your rune pouch in the center of the casting cloth, and light any candles or incense. If you'd rather diffuse oils, that works, too. Call upon any spirits you wish to invite. When the space and the vibe feel good, close your eyes and take a few deep breaths.

As you inhale, feel the air clearing your mind, heart, and body. Feel your breath oxygenating your blood and awakening your mind. Exhale distractions, doubt, fear, and tension. If you wish, sing an offering of your voice to the runes: A simple intonation will do, or you could chant the rune names. Your voice serves to center your body in the setting of the reading and to greet and introduce yourself to the runes in the ritual context. Ground yourself by imagining that your feet and your spine reach like tree roots into the earth. Try to feel the earth's heartbeat. Feel the sun and moon activating the crown at the top of your head. Open the palms of your hands upward so you are ready to receive. When you feel settled, it's time to begin your runecasting.

CAST YOUR RUNES

There are two ways to cast runes. The first is to literally cast out the runes upon the cloth and read all that lay faceup according to their orientation and relative placement. This must be done intuitively by a reader who has a well-ingrained understanding of the runes and can navigate a complex and chaotic spread without losing the threads of the story. If you cast by this method one day, you will already know in your heart how to do it. No book can teach it.

The second, and far more straightforward, method is to select a set number of runes for reading in a spread formation. You will choose a layout, then select runes one at a time to fill the various positions, each of which correlates to a specific detail of the overall question.

The Three Norns Spread (see page 44) is a great starting point, as it is versatile enough to address most questions and is stackable for reading on multiple parallel topics simultaneously. Spreads based on the Nine Worlds of Yggdrasil; the 12 zodiac signs or calendar months; the four seasons, elements, or directions; and other frameworks contextualize and clarify the runes' messages by filtering them through tried-and-true patterns.

Before selecting your runes, attune to them by speaking your question aloud while either moving them about facedown on your casting cloth or stirring them in their pouch. Make a note of any runes that flip over during this conversational shuffling phase, as well as what you were thinking or saying at the time, and interpret them accordingly before returning them to the pool. Decide what spread will best address your question, give the runes one more good shuffle, and pull one rune for each spread position (although if multiple runes really want to share one spot, listen). Announce the spread position and decide which end is up before revealing each rune in order to avoid the temptation to put them where you *want* them to be rather than where you *intuited* they should go.

Regardless of your level of knowledge and experience, always do your best to interpret runes from your head, heart, and higher self before looking them up in a reference. You may be surprised at what you pick up intuitively. Plus, the more you practice *reading* runes, the sooner it will start to feel natural. Journal your interpretations. After events have progressed, reflect on them and make notes on how your interpretation panned out or could have been improved.

When your reading is complete, thank the runes and any spirits you may have called upon. Return your runes to their pouch, put out any candles, and if you cast a circle or any sort of magical boundary, formally open or dismiss it. In the coming days and weeks, be sure to weave the wisdom of the runes into your daily choices, actions, and habits. If you continue to ask questions but do not implement the answers in your behavior, the runes may stop speaking to you because it seems you aren't listening. The runes can help you find your path and stay on track, but it is better not to seek their counsel than to hear and ignore it.

Reversed Runes

Not all runes can be reversed, and not everyone treats runes that have been reversed (merkstave runes) as significant. Thorsson says these "murky" staves must be read in relationship to their surrounding brighter staves and interprets them as either destructive or obstructive. Aswynn suggests interpreting merkstave runes as either the opposite or the absence of the rune. There are at least as many ways to read merkstave runes as there are rune readers. In my own readings, they have indicated that the action of the rune was blocked, misdirected, tempered, or lessened or that the rune's usual meaning was to be read in a negative, challenging, counterproductive, or weakened context.

Don't feel like you can't read runes because you don't understand merkstave runes (many rune readers ignore them). However, you must choose before you draw your runes whether you will read merkstave runes. Listen to your intuition and to the whispers of the runes, and you will know what to do.

DESIGN YOUR OWN TALISMAN

If you can create a bindrune or a runescript (see pages 28 to 29), you can create a talisman. Carve a runescript into the side of a pencil with an X-Acto knife, add a bindrune to the back of a pendant, or make a new piece of jewelry incorporating one or more runes. You can create a runic talisman using any method employed to make a set of runes, and you can alter almost any craft to incorporate runes, turning it into a talisman of sorts.

You can write runes on just about anything. I wear rune beads in my hair and write runes inside my wallet and shoes. The most important thing is to focus on the intention. If you have a last-minute need, remove one or more runes from a set to carry with you as a temporary talisman. Be sure to cleanse and return them to the pouch afterward.

You can charge runes by similar methods regardless of where they appear and what they are intended to do. If you trace out the runes with a wand or fingertip while intoning ALU or their names and sounds, you give the runes on your DIY talisman purpose, life, and breath.

CHAPTER

5

NAVIGATING RUNE SPREADS

This chapter introduces the use of spreads. We cover how to choose a spread and customize your own, then we delve into the specifics of an assortment of spreads you can use to peer into the unknown. Each spread is accompanied by a sample reading that demonstrates how the spread functions and shows how the individual meanings can shift and change depending on their context and position within a spread.

When you are first getting to know the runes, practice reading with these spreads in ascending order of complexity. Not every reading needs to address a major life decision, and if you want to become proficient, you will need to practice frequently before considering big issues. Start by conducting readings on low-stakes questions, such as weekend and dinner plans. Familiarity with the runes and spreads will pay off when you need them for more pressing questions.

CASTING SPREADS, GLEANING ANSWERS

The runes speak in rather abstruse terms, and they can be difficult to interpret without context. Spreads offer that context by providing micro-questions thoughtfully arranged into a visually evocative layout. During a reading, you select and place runes in positions within a spread. The position of each rune tells you how to interpret it relative to the question at hand. As a rule, more complex spreads can help clarify more complex situations, and simpler, smaller spreads are better for addressing more focused questions.

Some traditionalists argue that reading with spreads is a tarot technique that should not be part of rune readings, but our best historical account indicates that lots were selected in groups of three and interpreted accordingly. The great variety of spreads, regardless of their origins, is useful for casting and interpreting runes today. Norse mythology provides several archetypal frameworks you can transform into spreads for divination. The most obvious are the Three Norns and the Nine Worlds. Some spreads are based on other occult traditions, while others, such as the Challenge-Approach Spread, are designed for purely practical purposes. When you have mastered the basics of reading with spreads, you will be able to customize and create your own spreads for the unique questions and situations you and your querents bring to the table.

Óðinn's Eye

Óðinn's Eye is essentially a one-rune spread that comprises a single expression of the most fundamental unit of a rune reading: one micro-question, one position, one rune. According to myth, Óðinn gouged out his eye and placed it in Mímir's well in exchange for wisdom, but you will metaphorically attune your inner vision to the wisdom of a higher source. As you select a rune for this reading, you can visualize yourself removing your third eye and placing it in Mímir's well, which represents the innocence and ignorance you sacrifice when seeking knowledge and wisdom. By acknowledging this sacrifice, you accept responsibility for the knowledge and wisdom you will gain, and for the choices you make after receiving that knowledge and understanding. When your eye takes in the wisdom of the well, select a rune. That rune is what your third eye sees, and it is your job to interpret and apply its wisdom.

Only a single rune will respond, so for this type of reading to work, your question *must* be specific, clear, and concise. For example, if I am quarreling with someone, I might ask, *"What lesson can I integrate now to help resolve this quarrel?"* I might draw Hagalaz, the rune of hail, which symbolizes destructive and disruptive forces of nature. But as frozen hail melts into water and quenches the earth's thirst, the destruction Hagalaz augured eventually breeds rebirth and fertilization. I might step back and give the ice some time to melt before considering whether I learned anything valuable about myself or the other person as a result of this experience.

Óðinn's Eye is ideal for getting bite-size pieces of wisdom in a stand-alone situation, but this spread is also useful for tacking on to other spreads or readings to ask clarifying or additional questions.

"Both Sides, Now"

This spread was inspired by the Joni Mitchell song "Both Sides, Now." The song examines complementary perspectives and covers the gamut from clouds to love and life itself, and the spread is great for addressing topics where understanding two complementary perspectives is helpful to finding resolution.

The concept is simple: Ask for insight on two complementary issues, then draw two runes, one at a time, and place them side by side. The order doesn't matter as long as you know which side you're choosing each one for. The two things could be political parties, sides of a personal dispute, pros and cons of a particular job offer or career choice, or expectation versus reality—the dichotomies are endless. When you select the runes for this spread, focus on opening your perspective beyond your current understanding.

For example, my friend Kara was feeling called to get in touch with some old friends she hadn't spoken to in years. She wondered whether it was a good idea, and what the risks and benefits of reconnecting might be. We framed the question in terms of a cost-benefit analysis and pulled two runes: Uruz merkstave for cost, and Raiðo for benefit.

Uruz indicates that, like anything else, reconnecting takes time and energy, and possibly hints at the possibility that one or more of these old friendships could be energetically draining. Uruz merkstave is also a rune of shaping, and represents the lack of control Kara has over whether these relationships develop. On the other hand, Raiðo indicates that the urge to reconnect is an integral part of her greater journey, so over the long run, taking this step will move Kara forward on her path. Raiðo could also indicate the possibility of future travel, perhaps for Kara to reconnect with her friends in person.

Other variations on this theme, such as pros and cons or blessings and challenges, could help answer the question, *"What are some things I may not have considered about taking this job?"* or *"What are the likely consequences of staying in this relationship?"* The micro-questions come about by combining the spread positions with the relevant question. For example, the micro-questions that would be asked of each rune in those readings would be, *"What are some pros/good things I might not have considered about taking this job?"* *"What are some cons/bad things I might not have considered about taking this job?"* *"What blessings can I look forward to if I stay in this relationship?"* and *"What challenges can I expect if I stay in this relationship?"* Your intention is not to get the runes to decide for you. Each pair of questions is designed to get you closer to making the right decision for you.

Three Norns (Past, Present, Future)

This three-rune spread is perhaps the most traditional, as it is the only one even hinted at in historical accounts. The positions are most often attributed to the three Norns (or Nornir), the maiden giantesses who stand at the foot of the world tree tending the Web of Wyrd and ruling the destinies of gods and mortals. Their names are Urðr, Verðandi, and Skuld. *Urðr* is the past tense of the Old Norse verb "to be" and means "that which has already come to pass." *Verðandi* is the present participle of the same verb and means "that which is becoming/happening." *Skuld*, on the other hand, is derived from the Old Norse word for "that which ought to be/that which should/needs to happen." Skuld is the youngest Norn, and she is often depicted wearing a veil.

The added layer of cause and effect in the Three Norns Spread emphasizes natural consequences in a way that a standard past-present-future spread does not. The Urðr rune shows what happened in the past to shape the situation at hand. What Urðr shows cannot be changed, although sometimes you can reshape your attitude toward past events in ways that are almost as effective as altering the past. The Verðandi rune shows what is happening and coming into being. The forces described by the Verðandi rune are already set in motion, but they can often be tempered or trained somewhat to affect the probabilities of various outcomes. The Skuld rune shows what will likely come to pass based on the forces already set in motion.

With this spread, your overall question can be a little less specific, so it's a great go-to for querents who are curious about a particular topic but don't have a solid question.

For example, I might ask of my runes, *"Help me better understand my relationship with my mother."* When I actually did this reading for myself, I pulled Othala in the Urðr (past/became) position, Isa and Ingwaz together in the Verðandi (present/becoming) position, and Perthro in the Skuld (future/need/consequence) position.

Othala is the rune of family and inheritance, and under Urðr it references all I have inherited from my mother. I descended from my mother's body, and I inherit much of myself from her. Like most things that come up in the Urðr position, it's a part of my past that will forever shape my future. (That's fine, because my mom's awesome.)

Isa is a rune of ice and freezing and stillness, even immobility and stagnation. When pulled with other runes, it often indicates that the rune it is paired with is stuck or frozen.

Ingwaz is the seed of potential and stored energy, and is a fertility rune. As a fertile woman, I have the option to continue the work of my ancestors by passing their DNA into the future. That's not really on my radar right now, which is why Isa is paired here.

Perthro is the punch line of this little cosmic joke because it is the rune of the womb and the mystery, the lot cup, probability, and uncertainty. On the one hand, it seems to literally indicate birth, and indeed the cycle of maiden-mother-crone has continued unbroken from my most ancient ancestors, so it flows naturally that it should continue through me; sometime in the future, I may have a child and continue the cycle. In the future or outcome position of a reading, Perthro in all other contexts would typically mean "What will be will be" or "Who can say?" When I drew the Perthro rune for this reading, it felt like a double entendre. The runes are both stating a likely future outcome *and* refusing to tell.

My mom has definitely hinted that grandkids are high on her list of priorities, but this reading affirms that she knows it needs to be my decision (and my husband's, of course). This reading is a great example of how broad, general questions often lead to broad, general answers. If I wanted more specific information, I could have asked a more specific question. Instead, I was reminded of the cyclical nature of motherhood, which is worthwhile in itself.

Challenge-Approach

The Challenge-Approach Spread is a linear divinatory method of examining problems and generating positive solutions. The four runes in this spread are laid out from left to right and represent the following:

1. What the querent brings to the challenge
2. The nature of the challenge
3. A way to approach the challenge
4. The likely result of that approach

This spread is designed to suggest an approach to a problem and explain why it might be a good or bad idea, so you don't need to refine your question much more than that. You just need to focus on the situation at hand.

For example, if I've fallen behind in a project for school or work and I need help figuring out how to move forward with it, I could use this spread to seek counsel. I'll focus on the project at hand, keep the spread fresh in my mind, and select four runes.

If I select Uruz, Sowilo, Jera, and Tiwaz, I understand the following:

From Uruz: I bring a certain amount of creative energy and drive to this project. I will need energy and willpower to move through this project successfully.

From Sowilo: The challenge is to create at my usual standard but in a shorter time period. I need to summon a large burst of productive creative energy without sacrificing much in the way of quality. Sowilo portends success, but it often comes suddenly and at a significant cost.

From Jera: Because Tiwaz in the fourth position is positive, I can assume that Jera indicates a piece of advice I *should* follow to be successful, rather than a cautionary tale. This means that while my temptation is to dedicate every free second to this project so as to give it the maximum amount of time, it is still *really important* that I take regular breaks to clear my mind and move my body. If I focus on productivity at the expense of self-care, the quality of my work will suffer along with my health. Jera also reminds me that I reap what I sow, and there's room to interpret it here as a bit of an admonition, which is not entirely unfair.

From Tiwaz: The goal of my project is to share knowledge with the greater community, so Tiwaz in the outcome position is a great omen. One way to understand Tiwaz is the light of truth and knowledge shining down on the people, so this tells me that as long as I honor my cycles, I can still create what I need to for my project and it will still be able to achieve its purpose. However, there's also a sense in which these runes say that the *right* thing to do would have been to plan properly for the harvest I wanted to reap.

This was a really helpful reading, because while it all makes sense when put that way, the counsel is counterintuitive for me. When I'm behind in something, my tendency is to give it everything and not look away until it's done. These runes warn me that this approach will only lead to burnout and that I need to respect the cyclical natures of energy, creativity, and productivity to achieve the desired end.

Nine Worlds of Yggdrasil

According to Norse cosmology, the universe is understood in terms of nine separate worlds, all connected by the roots, trunk, and branches of the one world tree, Yggdrasil. Miðgarðr, literally "middle earth," is depicted at the center and is the world we know as home. The other eight worlds can be organized into four opposing pairs with complementary natures. Niflheimr and Múspellsheimr are the primordial worlds of ice and fire. It is said that where these two worlds touch is where life began. Jötunheimr is the wild and untamed land of the giants (Jötnar); Vanaheimr is the similarly wild but fertile and fair land of the Vanir, the

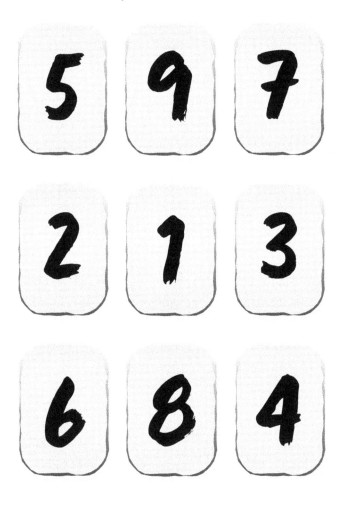

old nature gods (Freyja, Freyr, and their father, Njörðr). Svartálfaheimr and Ljósálfaheimr are the realms of the dark and light elves, respectively. Helheimr is the realm of the dead who did not die in battle, and Ásgarðr is the realm of the Æsir (Óðinn, Thor, Frigg, and others).

Most rune readers have a version of this spread; I use this one. Viewing any complex situation through the framework of the Nine Worlds will help you find clarity and hidden solutions. In this reading, nine runes correspond to the Nine Worlds, with Miðgarðr in the center synthesizing the surrounding runes. The natures of the worlds' corresponding spread positions are as follows:

1. **Miðgarðr** represents the querent, synthesizes the outer runes, and may indicate a possible outcome.

2. **Niflheimr** represents that which is stagnant, frozen, or inactive.

3. **Múspellsheimr** represents that which is active and in motion.

4. **Jötunheimr** represents that which challenges or goes against you.

5. **Vanaheimr** represents that which aids and supports you.

6. **Svartálfaheimr** represents your basic material or deeper subconscious motivations.

7. **Ljósálfaheimr** represents your thoughts, ideals, and conscious motivations.

8. **Helheimr** relays a message from your ancestors.

9. **Ásgarðr** relays a message from the divine.

When I did a reading for Ash, who was considering leaving a toxic family situation to live on his own for the first time and feeling both excited and afraid to be independent, I drew Tiwaz, Kenaz, Othala, Fehu merkstave, Dagaz, Elhaz, Isa, Berkana, and Ehwaz. This was my interpretation:

Tiwaz in **Miðgarðr** indicates Ash's self-perception as a pillar of support within his family. This is hopeful, because although he is nervous about living independently, it shows he already *knows* he can support himself *and others*. Only the context is unfamiliar.

Kenaz in **Niflheimr** makes sense because Ash's creativity has been stifled while living with his family. Gaining his own space will free Ash's creativity, which is necessary for his mental health.

Active in **Múspellsheimr, Othala** is the boundary around the family. In Ash's case, that boundary is toxic and stifling, and it needs to be redrawn.

Fehu merkstave in **Jötunheimr** indicates that Ash's challenge is financial. Money has been and will likely continue to be the biggest obstacle to leaving home.

However, **Dagaz** in **Vanaheimr** indicates mysterious divine forces supporting him as well as the positive self-transformation that will surely occur as a result of moving out. Dagaz is literally the dawn and metaphorically a door. Ash is guided to keep walking his current path right out the door, into the light of a new day and a new beginning.

Elhaz in **Svartálfaheimr** points to Ash's need to feel physically, mentally, and emotionally safe. This emphasizes the urgency of the move as well as the need for protection in the meantime.

Isa in **Ljósálfaheimr** indicates that Ash's primary conscious motivation is to be alone and independent, and to learn who he is when he's free to be himself.

From **Helheimr**, Ash's ancestors send **Berkana** as a reminder of their support and the importance of self-care.

Finally, **Ehwaz** in **Ásgarðr** is an omen of peace and harmony. In this position, Ehwaz both *advises* harmony (try to get along with others even as you walk away) and *predicts* it (Ash is likely to find the peace he craves soon).

A reading like this can help articulate what you already know but have not been able to clearly express. When you understand yourself explicitly, you are able to state your needs and desires explicitly, and everything you can speak, name, and identify, you can begin to call upon or create.

Wheel of the Year

The Wheel of the Year is an extremely versatile spread. The general concept is that you can ask one or more micro-questions about each segment of the upcoming year. The questions are customizable, and you can split up the year any way you like. You could divide it into four seasons and ask up to six questions about each (although fewer questions is probably more practical); eight sections divided along the solstices, equinoxes, and cross-quarter days, with up to three questions each; or 12 months or signs of the zodiac with up to two questions each. You could even do this reading for moon cycles or parts of a moon cycle. For the sake of brevity, the following example uses the four-part wheel.

My friend Embla has asked for a general reading about the upcoming year, so we asked the runes to indicate a blessing and a challenge for each of the coming seasons. You can use this spread anytime, although annual milestones are especially good. Embla is a college student who has just celebrated her 21st birthday, so this is a great time to use this spread for her. At the time I performed the reading, we were on the cusp of spring, so I began there and selected the following runes:

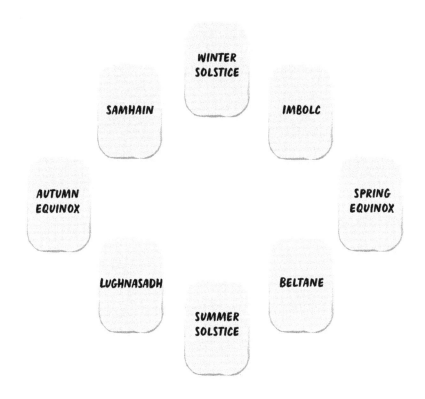

	SPRING	SUMMER	AUTUMN	WINTER
BLESSING	Hagalaz ᚺ	Laguz ᛚ	Jera ᛋ	Elhaz ᛉ
CHALLENGE	Uruz ᚢ	Fehu ᚠ	Raiðo ᚱ	Tiwaz ᛏ

For **spring**, **Uruz** as a challenge indicates that Embla may feel short on energy this season, possibly as a result of sickness, stress, or lack of sleep. **Hagalaz** heralds positive change following challenges, so being forced to slow down may be a blessing in itself.

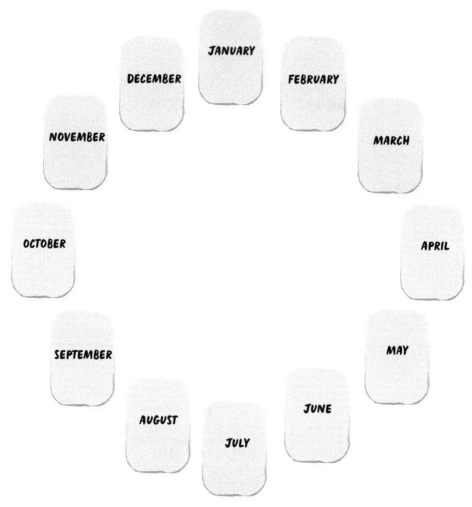

Summer foreshadows financial challenges with **Fehu**, but such is the life of a college student. The blessing is **Laguz**, or good physical, mental, and emotional health. Although funds may feel tight, Embla can rest easy knowing she has everything she really needs.

Raiðo as **autumn's** challenge indicates Embla may have trouble staying on the path she's committed to, but **Jera** reminds us that future harvests depend on present labors, and balance is necessary to maintain order.

In **winter**, **Tiwaz** presents a similar challenge to that of Raiðo, but this time it's one of willpower to uphold high standards. Winter's blessing is **Elhaz**, protection, so it seems Embla is protected from the worst of it, whatever that may be.

When time and circumstance give you a better idea of what these challenge runes indicate, you will have a better idea of how the blessing runes can help you navigate them, but you derive this benefit only if you come back to the reading throughout the year. This is why journaling is such an important aspect of rune readings.

LIVING THE RUNES

There are plenty of ways to incorporate the runes into your daily life beyond divination. One of my favorites is to create a runic calendar by assigning two runes to each month and keeping a journal reflecting on how I observe the runes in my life during their assigned month. For example, in January I might pay special attention to Fehu and Uruz, studying and reflecting upon their meanings and presence in the world. I recommend assigning the runes in order the first year and doing a Wheel of the Year Spread in subsequent years to mix it up.

Stadhagaldr, also called "rune yoga," is a postural runic practice developed in early 20th-century Germany. Some people find this helps them focus on the energy of a particular rune, and stadhagaldr sequences may be helpful for activating rune formulas like runescripts and bindrunes or for daily meditation and movement. You can practice this intuitively by creating the shapes of the runes with your body, or research the methods Karl Spiesberger and Edred Thorsson recommend (see Resources, page 126).

Many practitioners prefer to connect with the runes through chanting and intonation, and runic incantation can help move energy through the body and give vibration to intention. Sometimes I compose affirmations that include words with initial sounds corresponding to relevant runes, such as *"I am open to possibility"* for harmonizing with **Perthro**.

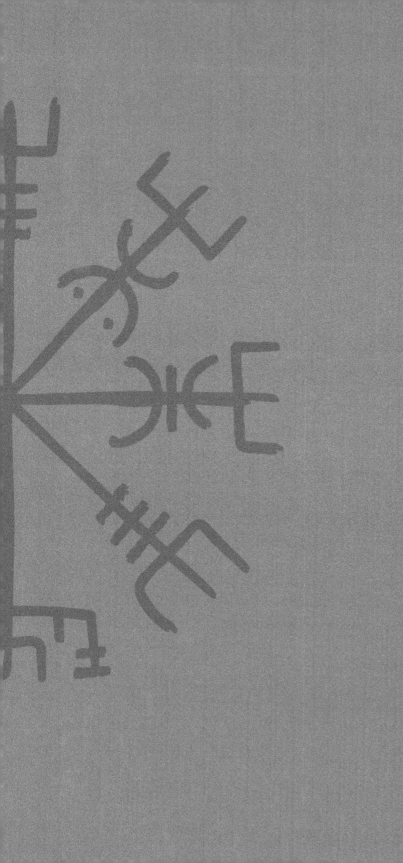

READING RUNES TODAY

The following chapters concern the Elder Futhark, the most ancient and most commonly used in modern magic. The Elder Futhark is divided into three *ættir* (groups of eight), each of which is thought to be governed by a particular Norse deity. There is no historical basis for these correspondences, and they are not unanimously agreed upon, but many modern practitioners find them helpful. The assignments in this book are not uncommon, and I use them in my practice.

The names of the runes in this book are from the reconstructed Proto-Germanic. They are historians' best approximations of what the names of the Elder runes would have been in the native language of their originators. Each rune is accompanied by its pronunciation, alternative names, translation(s), keywords, and layers of mystical meaning. For each rune, you will also find examples of how to interpret it within a reading, how to use it in spellwork and ritual, and how to apply its wisdom to a modern magical life.

As you read the following chapters and get to know the runes, keep in mind that there are things I do not know and things I cannot know. Much of my knowledge and understanding of the runes comes from historical documents and the writings of other rune authors, but a great deal derives from my own intuition and experience. Apply what resonates with you, examine what challenges you, and explore what makes you curious.

CHAPTER

THE FIRST ÆTT

The first ætt of the Elder Futhark is associated with the goddess Freyja. Freyja is lady of the Vanir and goddess of gold, fertility, love, war, and magic. Freya Aswynn (the author, not the goddess) explains how this ætt narrates the beginning of the universe from the appearance of the great cosmic cow Auðumla through the origins of the Jötnar and the Æsir up to the creation of the first humans.

The runes in this chapter are full of fiery and creative ecstasy. They are well suited for doing creative magic; building, repairing, and reinforcing interpersonal relationships; and expanding your own magic and wisdom. Let the journey through the futhark begin!

FEHU

Pronunciation: FAY-hoo

Also Known As: Fé, Feoh

Sound: F as in "father"

Translation: Cattle, wealth, fee

Keywords: Money, movable resources, wealth, cattle, gold, controlled energy, currency, generation, productivity, growth, investment

MODERN MEANINGS

Visually, Fehu is thought to depict the horns of domestic cattle. Although not many people trade in cattle these days, cattle were one of the primary forms of movable wealth for the Old Norse. In fact, the word *capital* is derived from the same origin as *cattle*. The most obvious form of currency today is money, and in readings, Fehu often refers to money. However, currency includes any goods you have or can make, any labor you can do, and any energy you can expend.

You can see the shape of Fehu in antlers; in the branching of plants, trees, and fingered limbs; and in the way your choices branch into alternate paths and possibilities. Fehu is also the currency of the life force itself. Fehu's natural tendency is to branch and multiply, whether in cattle, money, vitality, or crops. Fehu is generation and productivity. When invested and invested *in*, that which Fehu represents is fruitful and multiplies.

When Fehu appears merkstave (reversed), it may indicate that a flow of energy or currency is blocked. It is important to remember that flow goes both ways. Water must first flow *into* a pitcher to be poured out later. Similarly, if we do not get enough sleep, water, or healthy food, we will not have energy to invest in our goals, and spending money without generating income is unsustainable. The inverse of this blockage (too much coming in, not enough coming out) is also toxic, as those who hoard and stockpile resources will often watch their hoard rot or go to waste while those in need suffer.

Practical Magic

Fehu can be invoked for vitality, fertility, abundance, growth, and productivity. It can certainly be used to aid conception, but its uses are not limited to such ends. Call upon Fehu alone or with Kenaz to ensure fertile ground for ideas and creativity; with Gebo and Jera to empower an investment of money, time, or energy to give good returns; or with Berkana and Jera to encourage your garden to produce a bountiful harvest and plenty of seeds for next year. Fehu is also a vitality rune (although not as wild in nature as Uruz), so you can use it in glamour magic (with or without Uruz or Mannaz, depending on your intention) to make the wearer appear (or become) healthier and more fertile, which is essentially the same as appearing (and therefore becoming) more attractive.

Fehu is sacred to Freyja, as are cattle and gold. Freyja is the Norse goddess of wealth, love, beauty, and magic, and she is one of the deities associated with death and war. As Queen of the Valkyries (see Elhaz), Freyja selects half of those slain in battle to live on with her after death at Fólkvangr. Fehu is appropriate to invoke when making dedications, prayers, or sacrifices to Freyja, or when requesting her blessing (or the blessing of her brother, Freyr) upon your work.

FEHU IS YOUR FINANCIAL FRIEND

Write Fehu on the inside of your wallet, the corners of your bills, and your bank statements, or incorporate it into your signature when you endorse checks before depositing them. If you keep a piggy bank or have a mason jar savings account, paint or write Fehu on it. Invoke Fehu every time you send money, energy, or other resources in hopes it will stimulate the economy and spread abundance wherever it goes.

URUZ

Pronunciation: OO-rooz

Also Known As: Úr

Sound: U as in "true"

Translation: Aurochs, drizzle, rain, slag

Keywords: Strength, vital energy, manifestation, shaping energy, formation, crystallization, wild, energetic, untamed, virility

MODERN MEANINGS

Uruz is the primal life force energy, vital strength, and the power of formation. This rune's names are translated variously as aurochs, drizzle, rain, or slag. The aurochs were huge long-horned cows, the wild ancestors of domestic cattle, and were known for their raw power and energy. According to Norse mythology, Auðumla was a female aurochs who existed at the beginning of time as a result of the coming together of ice and fire. She nourished the giant Ymir (from whose body the world was made) with rivers of milk, and licked away at the salty rime and ice, revealing Buri, Óðinn's grandfather. She carried out the process of shaping and manifesting the progenitors of the Jötnar and the Æsir, forming and bringing both into existence. Uruz is both the aurochs and the rime she licks, the mist and drizzle that exists in the space between ice and fire, and the force of creation and life-shaping that exists at the center of this space. The conflicts that divide the Jötnar and the Æsir from each other are nonexistent for Auðumla. As the maternal cow gives life and milk to all her children, clouds bring rain to nourish the earth and all its creatures.

Uruz is active in the way your DNA tells your cells what to build, in the way pressure and the shape of a molecule dictate how it crystallizes, in the way your daily decisions shape the person you become, and in the way the arrangement of a room molds the activities within it. It is in the way vessels shape the fluids they hold, in the way artists move paint or shape clay, and in the way the shape of the land dictates the flow of water.

The slag referenced in one of the translations of this rune is the rocky waste by-product created during the process of refining raw metal ore. To create good, strong iron, you must remove the slag. To become the best and strongest versions of yourself, you must sacrifice your toxic habits and kiss your unhealthy patterns goodbye. In this way, the shaping power of Uruz is directed as a refining and purifying force.

In a reading, Uruz often refers to health. Its power is tied to the sacral and solar plexus chakras. When Uruz is healthy and active within, you know who you are and make decisions in alignment with your highest self. You are physically healthy, vibrant, and strong. When Uruz is unhealthy or inactive within (indicated by Uruz appearing merkstave or in a negative context), you may feel foggy and unsure about who you are. Your identity, beliefs, values, needs, and desires may be in question, and you may feel weak, tired, depressed, or directionless. You can activate and nourish Uruz energy in your body and in your life by getting proper rest, physical nourishment, and plenty of movement, and by making conscious decisions. Consciously considering your decisions forces you to ask yourself if they are in alignment with your goals, and although willpower is required to build good habits and make consistently healthy choices, the benefits for your mind and body far outweigh the effort.

Practical Magic

Uruz is almost a requirement for any manifestation magic performed with runes. Manifestation and many other types of magic depend on the caster's ability to exert the shaping power of their will onto their environment, thereby reorganizing reality according to their vision. Like most magic, it is just a poetic way of thinking about how your actions shape yourself and your environment.

Wear or carry Uruz on your person to increase willpower and remind yourself of the power of your every decision to shape reality. Uruz as an amulet or talisman may also help increase your vital energy for a period of time, but remember that you're borrowing against your future self.

Uruz can help you find a burst of energy when you really need it, but it can't generate endless energy for you.

RESHAPING REALITY

The same way sculptors shape lumps of clay and Uruz shapes the patterns of the world around us, psychologists have learned how to shape behavior. Lab rats, for example, are trained to perform complex tasks one tiny step at a time. If you want to train a rat to spin in a clockwise circle, start by rewarding the rat for every fraction of a clockwise turn, which encourages more of the same behavior. It's the same with people: If you want to encourage your roommate to help with the dishes, *do not* point out the soap bubbles clinging to the bottoms of the dinner plates they washed. Instead, thank them for their efforts, and in the future they'll be more likely to pitch in.

It's important to note that the changes you want to invoke in others' behavior start with changes in your own behavior—that is, your approach. When you remodel your world this way, invoke Uruz through visualization to empower your efforts magically.

THURISAZ

Pronunciation: THOO-ree-saz

Also Known As: Thorn, Thurs

Sound: TH as in "thorn"

Translation: Giant, thorn

Keywords: Thorn, destruction, defense, obstacle, barrier, pierce, penetrate, dispel, Thor, Mjöllnir

MODERN MEANINGS

The names of Thurisaz mean both "giant" and "thorn." For the ancient northern Europeans, both were destructive forces that posed threats and challenges. The giants (Jötnar) were the sworn enemies of the Æsir and embodied untamed natural forces (similar to the Greek titans). Thurisaz represents the challenges, threats, and obstacles the giants posed to the Æsir, but it also epitomizes the reactive, destructive force of Mjöllnir, Thor's hammer, which purportedly had the power to level mountains. The nature of Thurisaz is neither good nor evil. It is destructive and obstructive. It is both the challenge that would keep you from your goals *and* the weapon you use to destroy those challenges.

To argue good and evil over Thurisaz would be pointless, as it has no moral value out of context. Everyone has something to protect, and sometimes you will need to invoke its power. Thurisaz is not a mere shielding or sheltering type of protection, as it always has a piercing, disruptive, or destructive aspect to its nature. Elhaz is protection in the sense of a shield, a hedge, a roof, or shade; Thurisaz is protection in the sense of barbed wire, a thorny hedge, or a knight with a sword who has sworn to protect his ward.

When Thurisaz turns up in a reading, take note of what rune (if any) the thorn is pointing at and what rune (if any) is directly to its back, or protected by the thorn. Relative position can tell you a lot about what is being destroyed, challenged, or obstructed and what is being protected. Thurisaz merkstave can indicate weak boundaries or defense that backfires.

Practical Magic

When I first called upon Thurisaz, it manifested in my life as new and uncomfortable philosophical arguments that destroyed my entire worldview from the foundation, and it watched as I rebuilt my perspective from the ground up. It was difficult but necessary, and cleared the way for a new and better foundation. Awakening to consciousness is uncomfortable and sometimes painful, which is a strong motivation for some to dull their senses, but Thurisaz helps destroy the illusions that keep us from coming face-to-face with the truth and the nature of reality. Only when we see things as they truly are can we begin to heal them. Thurisaz can be a rune of healing, but it will rip the Band-Aid right off and will not coddle you. (For runic aftercare, see Berkana, page 108.) Invoke Thurisaz to protect yourself from unwelcome spirits, for immune support, and to break down internal resistance to positive change.

THORN BOUNDARY

Setting boundaries can be difficult, especially for empaths who feel the pressure of others' wants and needs to the detriment of their own health and happiness. To strengthen your boundary-setting abilities, wear or carry Thurisaz somewhere on your person. Know that although others may take your boundaries personally, that reaction is about them, not you. Your boundaries are there for your protection. If they can't respect that, you don't need to let them into your life.

ANSUZ

Pronunciation: AHN-sooz

Also Known As: Æsc, Óss

Sound: A as in "all-father"

Translation: God, Óðinn, mouth

Keywords: Inspiration, word, wisdom, speech, magic, incantation, Óðinn, the divine, the Æsir

MODERN MEANINGS

The words you speak are powerful magical spells, even if you don't think of them that way. Identifying and naming your needs, struggles, desires, and triumphs enables you to communicate to the universe and its population the natures and methods of your needs, failures, successes, and passions. Your ability to shape your realities hinges on your willingness to speak your truth and vision and honor your needs and feelings with your words.

Ansuz is the rune of the word—song, poetry, and storytelling. It is the rune of bardic or skaldic magic, and it is by the power of Ansuz that the mead of poetry bestows eloquence and inspiration. According to myth, the first two humans, Ask and Embla, were awakened by Óðinn, Vili, and Vé from two trees, an ash and an elm. The three brother-gods gave Ask and Embla the gifts of life, among them *Önd* and *Óðr*, roughly "breath" and "inspiration." These are the gifts of Ansuz. The magic of words and language is also the magic of the runes, for the runes are a symbol language themselves. Ansuz is the rune of the runes.

In a reading, Ansuz can indicate whether the power of your word goes for or against you. It may also appear as a call to action to claim your voice. If it appears in a position of excess, it may indicate that, like the boy who cried wolf, you have misused or overused your words to the point that you have devalued and disempowered them. Ansuz merkstave can indicate a blocked throat chakra, an unwillingness to speak up, or the misuse or abuse of the power of the word.

Practical Magic

Ansuz is tied to the throat chakra and the power of affirmations and mantras. Ansuz is the rune of charisma, speech, public speaking, and persuasion, and you can wear or carry it as a magical aid to inspire and empower speech. Some of the most powerful and transformative moments in life can be the moments we first claim certain titles for ourselves, such as the first time I called myself a witch. If there is someone or something *you know is you* (man, woman, witch, artist, feminist, conservative, writer, beautiful, funny, smart), name it and claim it. So often it is only imaginary gatekeepers and fear of judgment that keep you from claiming your identity and your power or using your words to speak your truth. Ansuz can help you overcome this. Invoke Ansuz to give your words extra power, especially when speaking your truth requires courage, strength, or inspiration.

OUR WORDS SHAPE OUR ATTITUDES

Some things, such as experiences, careers, and hometowns, are more pleasant than others, but the language you use to talk about them affects your relationship to them. When you shift your language to reflect that your circumstances are largely the result of your own choices, your attitude can shift to one of gratitude, and you can begin to feel empowered to push through the resistance and make changes. As an exercise, carry a charged Ansuz on your person for a day and make an effort to notice how your words reflect your attitudes, and perhaps how you can alter them to reflect healthier attitudes. Small changes in vocabulary can have far-reaching and powerful effects, and you might be amazed at how quickly you can convince yourself of alternative perspectives when you try.

RAIÐO

Pronunciation: RYE-though

Also Known As: Rad, Reið

Sound: R as in "ride"

Translation: Ride, journey

Keywords: Journey, ride, rider, right path, right action, wheel, spiral dance, rhythm, destiny

MODERN MEANINGS

The Anglo-Saxon Rune Poem says this of Raiðo: "Riding is a comfort to every warrior / in the hall, and very trying to those who sit upon / a powerful courser over the mile-paths" (Hostetter 2017). Raiðo is the journey, the rider, and the wheel. The nature of life is such that you experience your own journey in greater and more vivid detail than you will ever experience the journey of another person. This is what it means for a ride to look easy to the person who sits "in the hall," when the rider on the horse's back knows the ride is long, hard, tiresome, dangerous, and demanding. The nature of riding (and of anything) is also that you are riding on the backs of horses and standing on the shoulders of giants. You go nowhere fast alone, and it is worth asking who is bearing the burden of your progress with or for you.

Karl Spiesberger offers another perspective: Raiðo is the spiral dance, the cosmic world rhythm. The simultaneous forward and cyclical motion of the wheel is a metaphor for the spiral natures of life's lessons, the world's history, and your personal journey. You go around in circles, but you also evolve and move up the spiral as you traverse your life path. You may sometimes feel frustrated that it seems you are being subjected to the same lessons over and over, but it takes as long as it takes, and what matters is that you continue on your path for the entire length of your journey on this planet and do your best each day.

When Raiðo appears, it reminds you to focus on the journey rather than the destination. Raiðo may also appear to remind you that *methods matter*, and sometimes it is better to do the right thing than to win. Although it's good to know where you want to go and to try your best to get there, if the cost of getting there is your integrity, it's never worth it. It is better to compromise the dream than your integrity. Raiðo may also appear simply to let you know you're on the right track. It can also indicate a literal physical journey, from which Tony Willis extrapolates that it can also indicate a message from afar. Raiðo merkstave may indicate that you've gotten distracted and wandered off the path to your destiny. If this is how Raiðo appears to you, take a moment to consider whether you know where you're going and where you want to go, and if those are the same place.

Practical Magic

Raiðo is helpful as a talisman for perseverance, dedication to your path, and focusing on the (literal or metaphorical) road ahead. When short-term pleasures threaten long-term goals, call upon Raiðo to help you maintain focus and get assistance in making the right and responsible choices as you journey toward your destination. Raiðo is also a great rune to aid in travel, and a bindrune of Raiðo and Elhaz can help protect travelers.

ONE STEP AT A TIME

If you ever feel stuck or overwhelmed by the magnitude of the journey ahead, call on Raiðo and take a moment to be present on your path. When you feel as though you are running in circles and going nowhere, remember that the wheel spins in seemingly stationary circles thousands of times before reaching its destination. Progress is not always evident while it's happening. You can invoke Raiðo to help you be present through each step of your journey and move forward. You may not know what the next dozen correct decisions look like, but you can almost certainly figure out *one good thing* to do right now, today, to move one step in the right direction. Do this today, do this every day, and soon you will find that you are moving down your right path.

KENAZ

Pronunciation: KEH-naz

Also Known As: Kaun, Kauna, Ken, Kaunaz, Kaunan

Sound: K as in "kitten"

Translation: Torch (or sometimes ulcer)

Keywords: Knowledge, curiosity, exploration, illumination, light, fire, torch, forge, creative power

MODERN MEANINGS

Kenaz literally means "torch" and represents fire in its human-controlled forms. This includes the fire of creative inspiration and action, the fire of the hearth by which we create nourishment and comfort, the fire of the forge by which we shape raw materials into specialized tools, and the fire of the torch illuminating the darkness. As the torch we carry, Kenaz illuminates the world we know, the part of the path we can see. The brighter your light and the greater your curiosity, the more you can see; but the greater the area within your ring of light, the greater the perimeter bordering the known unknown. The old saying holds true: The more you know, the more you know you don't know. This aspect of Kenaz survives in the modern Scottish word ken, which means "know."

Kenaz is your creative will and exploratory curiosity. It is skill, craft, knowledge, and mastery. Uruz governs the shaping and formation of yourself from within, but Kenaz governs your power to know, master, and shape the environment and objects over which you have dominion and creative sway. This extends to skillful use of the runes and other magics, although Ansuz governs the magics themselves.

In a reading, Kenaz often refers to literal skills and mastery. Depending on context and its position in a spread, it may mean that your skills are needed and you are being invited to generate creative solutions and forge something new. Kenaz can refer to any skill or project you are passionate about. In certain contexts, Kenaz can also refer to the primal fires of Múspellsheimr. Other times, Kenaz is the active curiosity that seeks answers through conscious exploration. In this sense, it is the rune of the spiritual seeker *and* the sage, the dedicated apprentice *and* the practiced master.

Kenaz merkstave can indicate that your skills require refinement, you are out of practice, or your skill set is not suited for the task at hand. It may also indicate that you are exploring in the wrong direction and your quest for knowledge is a wild-goose chase, or your most valuable skills are being wasted. It is not good to ignore a calling. Creative individuals are sometimes tempted to ignore their inclinations in favor of more practical paths to success, but they often find that silencing their inner artists exacts a great price on their spiritual and mental health. Finally, Kenaz merkstave can indicate that your inner fire has gone out. This could be an indication of anything from a creative blockage to serious depression. (If you suspect something serious, please see a qualified professional—the runes can only reach so far.)

Practical Magic

Wear, carry, or draw Kenaz on your person to awaken your dormant creative powers, strengthen existing ones, or support your quest for knowledge, whether for an assigned research project or a topic of personal interest. Invoke Kenaz during daily practice sessions to strengthen your craft and hone your skill. Focusing on the hard C sound, chant the phrase "*I can*" to yourself, or create a more specific affirmation for yourself about what exactly you *can* do. The mystery of Ansuz is that our words have a funny way of transforming reality. "*I can practice guitar for ten minutes a day*" soon becomes "*I can play guitar!*"

TO LIGHT ONE CANDLE

When you deny or refuse your own creative power, you are cursing yourself to a destiny that others decide for you. To those who would complain, an old saying advises that it is far better to light one candle than curse the darkness. To wield the torch of Kenaz is to claim your creative power.

Without compromising fire safety, find a dark and comfortable space, a candle, and something to light it with. In the darkness, take a moment to acknowledge all the words and forces that try to take away your power, excuses you use to avoid claiming your power, and myths of your powerlessness. Acknowledge the fact that the darkness is real and you may never be able to illuminate (and thereby eliminate) it entirely. When you are ready to acknowledge that it is better to light your own flame than bemoan a lack of light, light the candle and say the following:

"As I light this candle, I, [your name], claim ownership of my creative power and accept responsibility for my part in shaping my lived experiences. From this day forward, I carry the fire of Kenaz in my heart; I am the artist, and my life is my art. So it is, and so it shall be. Alu."

GEBO

Pronunciation: GEH-bo

Also Known As: Gyfu, Geofu

Sound: G as in "gift"

Translation: Gift, generosity

Keywords: Reciprocity, gift, exchange, generosity, hospitality, sacrifice, relationship, contract, love, marriage, sexual union, gratitude

MODERN MEANINGS

Gebo means "gift," and governs all relationships, contracts, sacrifices, and exchanges. To the originators of the runes, the act of receiving a gift necessitated, without question, the reciprocal act of giving a gift in return. Therefore, Gebo represents the gift that is reciprocated, the sacrifice that is accepted (and the blessing that is given in return), the way we help those who have helped us, and the way others lift us up when we have done the same for them. At its core, Gebo represents a reciprocal relationship between two entities. It can be a friendship or a love between two people, a mutually beneficial business partnership, or even the way your home or your car takes care of you as long as you take care of it.

For a relationship to be balanced and healthy, it *must* be reciprocal. If one party is giving in excess of the other (financially, emotionally, or in terms of time and attention), the overly giving party will begin to resent the other for all they have taken, even though it was the giver's choice to give where it was not reciprocated. On the other side of the equation, those who drink from the communal pot but never fill it will soon find it empty. However, Gebo is *not* about accounting, tallying, and keeping track of every little detail, or about revenge and getting even. By the time you're keeping lists to prove the existence of an imbalance, you already have a problem you need to address. Instead of getting even, get clear—or just get out.

Gebo can also refer to Newton's third law of motion: For every action, there is an equal and opposite reaction. Actions have consequences, both magical and mundane. Think of the lines that cross in Gebo as two hands coming together in a handshake. If one person reaches out their hand and the other doesn't reciprocate, it's weird. You *feel* something uncomfortable in the air. Alternatively, if one person shakes hands like a limp fish or another person practically arm wrestles you, that's weird, too. Either way, there's an imbalance. The way your greetings, jokes, and conversations are (or aren't) reciprocated goes a *long* way toward telling you how welcome you are in a relationship or social situation. From the other side, the way you reciprocate (or don't) others' greetings, jokes, and conversations goes a long way toward telling them how *you* feel about *them*.

Gebo has horizontal, vertical, and radial symmetry, so it can't appear reversed or inverted. It can, however, appear in certain contexts that indicate its action is blocked, obstructed, challenged, overactive, underactive, or toxic, and that typically indicates an imbalance in a relationship, either between the querent and another person or between something the querent dedicates a lot of time to but doesn't get a lot of return on. An employer who says they really need you but doesn't respect your time or pay well is a good example of Gebo gone bad.

In a positive context, however, Gebo represents all that is good and right between and among lovers, friends, and colleagues. Gebo is the symbol of sexual union, true shared intimacy, and mutual love and respect. At its simplest, Gebo in a reading may refer to an existing relationship or more generally to the need to love and be loved. It might just mean the universe has a gift in store for you.

Practical Magic

Incorporate Gebo into any sacrifices you offer. If you burn a handwritten letter as an offering, draw Gebo in the corners beforehand. If you offer your gods an apple, carve Gebo into its flesh, along with any other runes that you deem appropriate based on the nature of the sacrifice and the blessing you seek. Gebo marks the sacrifice as a gift and acknowledges the rhythm of give and take.

Seal your love letters with a kiss by adding a few Xs near your signature. Many people know Xs signify kisses, but you'll invoke another layer of meaning in every little love note you write.

Gebo is helpful for seeking and strengthening healthy relationships (whether romantic, friendly, familiar, or professional), as well as in sexual magic.

THE LANGUAGES OF LOVE

Understanding how each of us prefers to give and receive love can take us a long way toward healthier, happier relationships and strengthen the positive action of Gebo in our lives. Sometimes both members of a relationship (whether romantic, platonic, familial, or professional) *are* giving, but because their love languages are not aligned, neither feels they are receiving enough love. In *The 5 Love Languages*, Gary Chapman identifies five primary modes of giving and receiving love: words of affirmation, quality time, gifts, acts of service, and physical touch. If a relationship doesn't feel reciprocal, try not to assume the other party doesn't care about your needs. It's more likely they don't know what your needs are, so take some time to communicate them. Invoke Gebo beforehand to seed the pattern of reciprocity in the conversation.

Once you know your primary love language, you will be better able to speak your needs, and the people who love you will be better equipped to meet them. If your relationships are already awesome, learning about and discussing your love languages can help fortify them for years to come. You can take Dr. Chapman's official quiz to determine your love language at 5LoveLanguages.com/quizzes.

WUNJO

Pronunciation: WOON-yo

Also Known As: Wynn

Sound: W as in "welcome"

Translation: Joy, perfection

Keywords: Community, that which brings people together, joy, bliss, wish, will, perfection

MODERN MEANINGS

Wunjo is the flag that brings people together. It is usually translated as "joy," which does bring people together in celebration. However, Aswynn translates this rune's name as "perfection" and likens its meaning to a pre-fall paradisiacal bliss. In this preconscious world, before we knew our shadows and understood our capacity to harm and be harmed, we existed in a state of perfect love and trust. Now that we have seen the darkness within ourselves, we can't unsee it, and we imagine its presence in everyone we meet. Can we ever return to that previous state of perfection? Ignorance is bliss, but knowledge is power. When Gebo is strong within a community or relationship, the bliss of Wunjo becomes possible within.

Another meaning of this rune is "wish." Óðinn is also associated with this rune, and one of his many roles is that of the fulfiller of wishes—think "wizard-god Santa." We wish for many things and strive for perfection despite our awareness of its impossibility. If your life is not shaped by your ideals, it is just a series of accidents, and you get what you are given. If you can identify your bliss, you can follow it to your destination and learn to say no to anything that doesn't align and yes to everything that does, thereby shaping your lived reality according to your image of perfection.

In a reading, Wunjo can represent an idea; a community; a common goal, purpose, or value; a wish; or a sense of oneness or blissful perfection. It may sometimes appear as a reminder to use the power of your will to further your vision. Merkstave, Wunjo can indicate that your values or ideals are skewed or not aligned with those of the people around you, or that your access to your vision or willpower is limited or blocked. Wunjo merkstave can also refer to suspicion, mistrust, or disharmony among friends or kinsmen. It can indicate domestic disputes, a lack of teamwork, a weak social network, a lack of shared values, or conflicting ideals or visions for the future. When Wunjo is overactive, it can manifest as the dissolution of the individual into the hive mind (as in a cult) or as someone who is so overconcerned with living out certain ideals that they lose their community by withholding grace (cancel culture).

Practical Magic

In magical workings, Wunjo is the wishing-rune. When doing any sort of wish spell, include and invoke Wunjo to empower the wish. Wunjo is a great rune to incorporate into gathering spaces or to invoke during group meals, get-togethers, and celebrations to invite joy, bliss, and togetherness into the atmosphere.

Invoke Wunjo to follow your bliss and aid in the mission to create heaven on earth. Wunjo can also strengthen leadership skills and help unite people toward a common cause.

PERFECT VISION

Through the power of your will, you imprint your visions onto the world around you, but to exert your will on anything, you must first know your will. To strengthen your will, first strengthen your vision. You may want a better world, a better life, or a better job, but what does that *look* like?

Journal about your visions and hopes for the future, then tear up magazines or print out pictures from the Internet and create a vision board of your ideal life. Before you start gluing things, inscribe a large red Wunjo in the center of your vision board and charge it, visualizing your version of a perfect world. (You may also add other runes, if you like.) Attach your images, covering the runes or letting them peek through. When your vision board is complete, hang it where you will see it every day, and let it remind you of your wish so you can act in accord with it.

CHAPTER

7

THE SECOND ÆTT

In this chapter, we meet the second ætt of the Elder Futhark, which is associated with the goddess Hela. She is goddess of death and the grave, and rules as Queen of the Dead in Helheimr (a cold, grim place). She is described as half fair young maiden and half decaying skeleton.

The first few runes in this ætt bring bitter cold, treacherous ice, and serious hardship, which make for a fitting introduction. Contrary to common misconception, however, Hela isn't evil. She merely enforces natural laws. Death isn't evil, it simply *is*. It is the necessary complement to life. The grave is merely the mirror of the womb. At the end, we return to the great mother. Because Hela embodies both life and death, her ætt contains summer and snow as well as the bridge between opposites. The runes in Hela's ætt are well suited for ancestral work, otherworldly travel, and weather magic.

HAGALAZ

Pronunciation: HA-ga-laz

Also Known As: Haglaz, Hægl, Hagall

Sound: H as in "harsh"

Translation: Hail

Keywords: Transformation, turbulence, manifestation, weather, random acts of god, order, crystallization, disruption

MODERN MEANINGS

Hagalaz, which means "hail," deals with the crystallization process at the center of hail's creation; the violent, turbulent, and often destructive effects of hail when it falls to earth; and the life-giving aftereffects of a hailstorm when the ice melts.

According to Norse cosmogony, at the beginning of time there was only ice and fire. They came together; the fire melted the ice, and the water droplets became Ymir, the first giant. Hagalaz is a rune of manifestation, crystallization, order, and new beginnings. When hail hits, it *hurts*. It ruins plans and can damage homes, vehicles, and personal property. It comes unexpectedly, and although you can protect yourself and many of your possessions, you cannot stop or divert it. But at its core (and throughout), hail is made of *water*, which is the source of all life. All living things must have water, and when hail melts, it brings the gift of water to earth from heaven. Thus, although Hagalaz represents unforeseeable obstacles, surprise challenges, and unfortunate acts of god, it also represents that which will revitalize and heal over time.

Just as a hailstorm might knock out your daffodils and then hydrate your herbs, when Hagalaz appears in a reading, it may indicate an event or occurrence that will at first bring challenges and seem like an obstacle but later prove beneficial. Hagalaz cannot appear merkstave, but in a negative position it may mean there are more storm clouds than silver linings. In a positive aspect, it may indicate that the current challenges will soon pass and the silver linings of your storm clouds will become clear.

In a future position, Hagalaz typically indicates an obstacle you cannot fully plan, calculate, or correct for.

When Hagalaz came up in a reading I did while planning my wedding, I figured we should expect it to rain and made peace with moving the spring ceremony indoors. The weather reports predicted thunderstorms nine days out, but eight days before our wedding, the World Health Organization declared COVID-19 a pandemic, and large gatherings were deemed illegal in my city shortly thereafter. Did we still get married? Yes. Was it anything at all like we had planned? No. Were there hidden blessings to be found in this freak event? Yes. And, in nature's typical comic fashion, *did it rain*? No. That's Hagalaz for you.

Practical Magic

Hagalaz was there at the beginning of the universe, and it is a good rune to have at the center of beginnings now. Ice crystallizes outward from a seed formation in the most efficient pattern possible according to the molecular structure of water. Invoke Hagalaz to encourage order and structure in your life. Be aware, however, that creating an ordered end product (such as healthy morning and bedtime routines, an organized study system, or an organized closet) often requires enduring a great deal of turbulence and upheaval at the outset. If you want the blessings of Hagalaz, you must be willing to play on its terms. If you cannot survive the hail, you will not be around to see the flowers.

Wear or carry a bindrune or runescript of Elhaz, Hagalaz, and Jera (if a runescript, in that order) to fortify yourself against the fallout of turbulent change and encourage your own resilience when such events transpire.

CRYSTALLIZED INTENTIONS

Through Hagalaz, you can combine the creation of a rune wheel or helm with the use of a crystal grid. Hagalaz-based helms are great for manifestation and solidifying your intent, and working with crystals can temper, season, or amplify your other magical practices. The icy appearance of quartz and its fairly neutral qi echo Hagalaz and will amplify but not interfere with your intentions.

Eight-spoked rune wheels such as Vegvísir or the Ægis-hjálmer were quite common historically, but using the six-spoked snowflake form of Hagalaz ᛝ as the center of a rune wheel invites its manifesting and ordering energy to crystallize your intentions outward. You will need something roughly flat on which to inscribe your rune wheel, something with which to inscribe it, and six natural quartz points. Choose one or more runes for the six spokes according to your purposes, and inscribe your rune wheel at an appropriate size for your crystal points (probably no smaller than 4 inches across). Place the quartz points on each of the six spokes of your rune wheel, pointing outward. You can add additional crystals to your grid, but be sure they align with your intent. When you are pleased with the arrangement, charge your rune wheel crystal grid the same way you would charge any other runic talisman (see page 26).

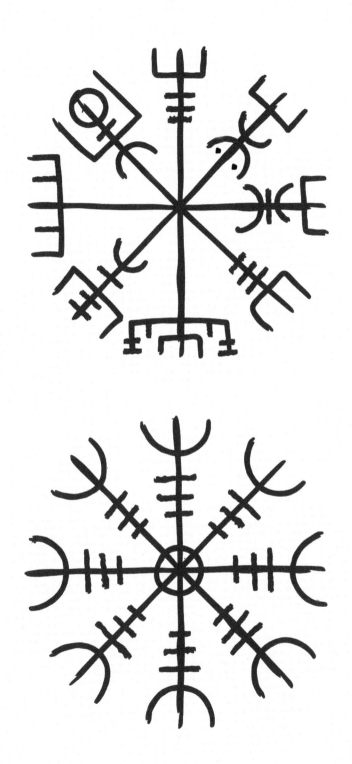

NAUDIZ

Pronunciation: NOW-these

Also Known As: Nauðr, Nyd

Sound: N as in "need"

Translation: Need, necessity

Keywords: Need, necessity, hardship, need-fire, sacrifice, cost, price, level up, inevitability, Skuld, emergency, necessity is the mother of invention

MODERN MEANINGS

Naudiz is literally "need" and "necessity." It is the need to sacrifice, the need to level up, the need to act. When everything is at stake and the question is posed, *"Do you have what it takes? Can you do it?"* Naudiz answers through your lips, *"I must. I have to."*

I asked my runes how to balance my umpteen priorities, and Naudiz said, *"You can't. Pick three."* It is a simple truth about space-time and the human brain that we can really focus on only one thing at a time. Often, we have to sacrifice something for something else to move forward.

I asked the runes to hold my hand and make my challenges easy, and Naudiz said, *"The challenges don't get easier. You just get stronger."* Sometimes you have to level up to move forward. It takes focus, energy, raw materials, and physical labor for wood to catch a spark and make a flame. Likewise, there is a cost for your ascension, and you must pay it in your own blood, sweat, and tears.

I asked the runes what would happen if I failed, and Naudiz said, *"You must not fail."* If Naudiz comes up when asking about alternative options, it may mean there *is* no other way.

I asked the runes, *"I know what the next step is, but how do I actually take it?"* and Naudiz said, *"You'd better figure that out, and quick."* Necessity is, after all, the mother of invention.

Like Skuld, the Norn of the future and *that which should be,* Naudiz governs the necessary consequences of past actions and events. In a reading, Naudiz indicates that whatever it refers to is not optional, but necessary. Naudiz may presage hardship, loss, or adversity, but typically such misfortunes are unavoidable acts of nature or necessary costs of other objectives, not punishments for poor choices. Naudiz cannot appear merkstave, but in a negative aspect can be particularly unfortunate. In a positive or neutral aspect, Naudiz often indicates that a certain sacrifice, austerity, or diligence is required to move forward favorably; this is not necessarily a bad thing, but rather a rite of passage.

Practical Magic

Naudiz can help you find the wisdom to make the right sacrifices. If you have a heavy course load and must drop something from your calendar, or your budget is tight and you have to choose between two options, carve Naudiz into a candle, light it, and focus on the flame or the shape of the rune while you meditate on the matter. Or you can do a full-on reading to ask the runes what you must sacrifice to gain what you desire or require. Place Naudiz at the top of your casting cloth to set the tone for your reading.

As the rune of that which should be, you can invoke Naudiz to run an audit of spiritual and natural consequences and start to set things right. But remember, this applies to you, too.

THE NEED-FIRE

Naudiz is the rune of the need-fire, the fire lit to make sacrifices and request what is needed. When you are truly in need, build your own need-fire. A small cast-iron cauldron and an instant coal will work, but an outdoor firepit with wood is better. Once your fire is lit, make your burnt offering. The offering should be something that represents what you are sacrificing from your life. If it is safe and makes sense to do so, you may burn the thing itself, but neither toxic relationships nor smartphone addictions can be safely or reasonably burned, so in most cases, you will want to burn a representation. A drawing, photograph, or page of writing will typically suffice, but feel free to get creative. Inscribe Naudiz on the offering and give it to the need-fire. Chant Naudiz as you do so or say a few words about why you are making the sacrifice.

If you make the appropriate sacrifice, the desired consequence will typically arise naturally. You don't have to ask for your desired outcome, but you can state it, and you must articulate what you want in order to know what to sacrifice. If you are making an offering *to* someone or something and asking for something in return, that sacrifice is governed by Gebo. If you are sacrificing something to make way for something else, *that* is governed by Naudiz.

ISA

Pronunciation: EE-sah

Also Known As: Is, Isaz

Sound: I as in "ski"

Translation: Ice

Keywords: Ice, frozen, stillness, stagnation, blockage, obstacle, inaction, stuck, winter, cold, independence, solitude, ego

MODERN MEANINGS

Isa is the cold and the stillness of ice. Ice freezes over rivers and roads and blocks access to needed resources, but it also creates bridges across bodies of water. Ice forms a slippery shield, preserving what is frozen within and deflecting what would approach from without. Isa is frozenness, stillness and stagnation, bitter cold and harsh winter. Stillness can be positive (meditation, healing, rest, reflection) or toxic (lack of growth and progress). Isa is the integrity and stillness of that which is frozen within or beneath the ice and the discouraging reality of living on the slippery surface. Isa is also the rune of the ego—it is "I," the identity and integrity of the individual.

In a reading, Isa usually indicates that something is frozen or blocked, or that it's time to slow down, stop, rest, and reflect. Look to surrounding runes to see what is affected. Alternatively, Isa may indicate a preservative or conservative force. Surrounding runes will indicate what must be preserved. Isa cannot appear merkstave, but will take on more austere meanings in negative contexts and lean toward its preservative and protective aspects in more positive positions.

Practical Magic

The primary uses for Isa magically are in preservative magic and protective/reflective/defensive magic. Meditate on Isa to create an ice-like energetic shield around yourself that deflects distractions, irritations, and counterproductive temptations. Invoke Isa to solidify connections, prevent movement, freeze chaos, bind or deflect hostile forces, fortify your will against temptation or provocation, or strengthen or preserve your individual identity.

ICE BINDING

There is a tradition of protective freezer spells that bind the words or actions of someone who is speaking or acting against you by freezing a symbolic representation. You can enact similar workings against toxic patterns or habits in your own behavior. First, write the full name or a description of the target on a piece of paper, then fold it up. If you are able to include a photo or additional symbols, even better. Inscribe the rune Isa on both outer sides of the folded paper and stuff it in a freezer jar. Fill the jar (leaving headroom) with snowmelt, spring water, or an appropriate crystal elixir (such as one made with clear or included quartz), and seal tightly. Inscribe Isa on the lid of the jar before placing it in the freezer. When the spell is frozen, so too will be the words and actions that once worked against you.

JERA

Pronunciation: YAY-rah

Also Known As: Jeran, Jeraz

Sound: Y as in "year" (can also be used to replace J as in "June")

Translation: Harvest, good year

Keywords: Year, harvest, summer, good year, good harvest, crop, cycle, thaw, wheel, time, progress

MODERN MEANINGS

Fundamentally, Jera embodies a good harvest. On a personal scale, Jera represents the consequences and rewards of past actions (you reap what you sow, what goes around comes around, and the like). On a communal scale, Jera is the summer—warmth, fresh fruit bursting with juice, the buzz of life and activity, abundant harvests, good times. On a cosmic scale, Jera is cycles—the cycle of the year, the moon cycle, the water cycle, historical and political cycles, weather cycles, and recycling. Jera is at the midpoint of the futhark and the top of the wheel of the year.

In a reading, Jera may indicate successful results, such as an indication that your efforts will pay off or already have. It can also literally refer to summer or next year, or mean "maybe next time." Sometimes it's just a reminder that you get out of most things roughly as much as you put into them, so you might want to step up your game.

Jera cannot appear merkstave, but in a negative context it can show up to explain why the work you didn't do before isn't paying off like you wanted it to, or it might mean your efforts are *not* paying off, in which case you had better take your good intentions elsewhere. Jera is usually positive, however, and serves as an indication of good things coming— either you will soon reap the juicy-sweet fruits of your labors or summer is coming to warm the earth. In addition to literal harvests, Jera governs annual merit-based raises, grades, the products of creative activity, the way children mirror and mimic their parents' behavior, and who we become based on our habits and routine.

Practical Magic

Whereas Isa is used to freeze, bind, and halt, Jera can be used to thaw, stimulate, and catalyze. Call upon Jera to get things moving when events are progressing too slowly or not at all. You can use Jera to stimulate yourself when things are getting dark and you're feeling stuck, although it doesn't replace professional mental health care. More generally, you can use Jera to enact your will slowly and steadily, which is typically much more effective than the get-it-quick spellwork that always sounds so appealing but hardly ever works.

GROWING THINGS

To connect with Jera, experience the life cycle of a plant from seedling to harvest firsthand. You can plant seeds yourself or purchase a young plant for your home. Herbs for your kitchen are rewarding and fairly easy, and I've always preferred growing plants I get to eat. Pick something that excites you.

Mark Jera on the surface of the soil near the base of your plant by scratching with a stick, arranging sticks or stones, or placing a charged stone or other talisman bearing Jera on the soil. As you care for the plant, periodically recharge the rune at its base. The plant and your relationship to it will reveal deeper mysteries of Jera to you.

If you have some experience caring for plants or if you're feeling particularly lucky, you can plant your intentions in the soil beneath your plant so your daily plant care becomes a long-term spell rather than a meditative practice. Bury a charged sigil, runescript, bindrune, or other talisman or meaningful object in the soil near the base of the container. Transplant your seedling directly over the buried talisman or spell paper. Tuck it in with soil and water and follow the same instructions described above.

EIHWAZ

Pronunciation: I-wahz

Also Known As: Eiwaz, Eihaz, Eoh

Sound: EI as in "Helheimr," either I as in "height," or possibly A as in "beige"

Translation: Yew

Keywords: Yggdrasil, yew, bow, ascension, transcendence, descent, vertical travel between worlds, world axis, bridge, integrity

MODERN MEANINGS

Eihwaz is the rune of the yew tree, which was known as the best source of bow wood for more than 7,000 years and is the best candidate for the species of Yggdrasil. Ancient yew trees are wondrous to behold. These words from J. R. R. Tolkien come to mind: "the old that is strong does not wither, deep roots are not reached by the frost."

Yew is one of the hardest of the soft woods. It is strong, yet springy and flexible. Whereas the strength of Isa is in its ability to freeze, harden, and preserve, the strength of Eihwaz is in its vitality, its springy flexibility, and its roots. Eihwaz is not brittle like ice; rather, it is strong *because* it is flexible and has some give. Eihwaz may appear as a reminder that you can maintain your integrity while your identity evolves. It serves as a reminder to stand tall but bend with the wind.

Yggdrasil is stated once in the Völuspá to be an ash tree but is repeatedly described as an evergreen conifer consistent with the characteristics of the yew. Additionally, the yew gives off volatile oils in the heat of summer that are toxic and could have contributed to the visionary initiation experience attributed to Óðinn on the world tree. As the spine of the world tree, Eihwaz is the rune of vertical travel between worlds. Inner journeys to upper and lower worlds such as the shadow plane or the astral plane are governed by this rune, as well as ascension within the self. Eihwaz is the vertical axis that unites the subconscious, conscious, and superconscious, for which the lower, middle, and upper worlds can be seen as metaphors.

Practical Magic

Wear or carry Eihwaz on your person when journeying to otherworlds within your mind or to strengthen your personal integrity. In addition to helping you stay true to yourself, Eihwaz can help you stay true to your goals and keep your eyes on the prize (Eihwaz on the Preihwaz?). As the rune of the bow, it seeks its targets swiftly and precisely.

Work Eihwaz into bindrunes or runescripts to maintain integrity within the working. A wheel of eight Eihwaz runes works well as a focus for meditative otherworldly journeys.

Because it bridges and connects the opposite upper and lower worlds of earth and sky, Eihwaz can be used to build or strengthen a connection between other sets of opposites.

BRIDGE TO ANOTHER WORLD

Take a guided journey to another world—inside your mind. The great expanse of the Internet is filled with guided meditations, and only by experiencing a journey to the upper and lower worlds can you really start to understand the meaning of Eihwaz. A good guided meditation will provide a repetitive soundtrack, take you through full-body relaxation, and offer suggestions for visualization that will enhance and inspire your journey. (For beginners, I recommend longer tracks with more guidance at the beginning and more freedom at the end.)

Some tips for these sorts of inner journeys:

- Have a clear question or goal, or else the journey becomes chaotic and directionless.

- Call on your guides and guardians beforehand to protect you.

- Relax fully. Any tension, even in your facial muscles, will keep you in the material world.

- If you feel like you're making it up, that's okay. You are exploring your own consciousness. You can receive valuable guidance and answers from parts of your consciousness you don't normally access.

- Remember, you are in charge. You can leave the journey at any time. If a figure makes you feel threatened or uncomfortable, you can command it to reveal its true form and refuse any requests it makes. You can also call upon your gods, ancestors, and other guides at any time. They are there to support you.

PERTHRO

Pronunciation: PEAR-thro

Also Known As: Peorth, Peorð, Perth, Pairthra

Sound: P as in "pear"

Translation: (unknown)

Keywords: Lot cup, dice cup, unknown, mystery, enigma, womb, birth, destiny, luck, Norns/Nornir, Schrödinger's rune, play, game, well or vessel

MODERN MEANINGS

No one actually knows the literal meaning of this rune, which is funny because that's what contemporary rune magicians have collectively decided it means. The only rune poem that mentions it, the Anglo-Saxon, calls this rune a source of recreation and group amusement, and many have interpreted the shape of the rune as a dice cup or lot cup for gaming. Some have theorized that the name of the rune (which does not appear elsewhere) refers to the wood of the pear tree, which may have been used to make game pieces, musical instruments, and other recreational objects, but this is all speculation. The rune's intended meaning may remain a mystery forever, but among contemporary practitioners, it is typically seen as a symbol of the mystery itself—the uncast lots, the unspilled beans, the darkness of the womb, Schrödinger's cat, the unseen future, the unknown facts, the undecided fortune. In short, Perthro represents that which you cannot know at this time.

In readings, Perthro typically indicates either that the answer you seek cannot be revealed to you at this time, or it relates to some sort of vessel, mystery, womb, probability, or game of chance. If the former, the universe may be undecided on the matter, or the information may be hidden from you for another reason. Merkstave, Perthro may indicate that the odds are not in your favor, or it may give a generally negative connotation to the implications of Perthro. It may also appear to remind you not to take anything (especially yourself) too seriously. The game of life is meant to be played with a sense of humor.

Practical Magic

You can call upon Perthro to ease pregnancy and labor for expectant and birthing mothers, especially in combination with Berkana. Perthro is also perfect to work with during any sort of rebirthing work or past-life regression (both of which involve metaphorically or ritually reentering and exiting the womb). On a more daily basis, wear or carry Perthro on your person to maintain a good sense of humor and flow with the universe's ever-changing plans.

Wear Perthro or carry it as a good-luck charm, or combine it with other runes to direct the flow of your luck. Create a bindrune of Perthro and Fehu for luck in money matters or Perthro and Ehwaz for luck in love.

SCHRÖDINGER'S RUNE POUCH

Any pouch, box, cup, or other vessel that contains a set of runes is essentially the material manifestation of Perthro. After all, you never know what may come out of it. To connect more deeply with Perthro, meditate on its shape while you apply it to your rune pouch, box, or lot cup, either by painting, embroidering, or some other method. Put a single stave on the front or underside of your vessel or create a decorative border or pattern of Perthro runes. Every time you draw or cast your runes from their vessel, you will reconnect with the mystery of Perthro.

ELHAZ

Pronunciation: EL-haz

Also Known As: Algiz

Sound: Z as in "Zen"

Translation: Elk

Keywords: Protection, shield, elk, elk-sedge, boundary, guardian, Valkyries, hedge, fence

MODERN MEANINGS

Protection is the common thread that runs through all the distinct meanings of Elhaz. Elk have antlers to protect them. Hedges have thorns for protection and to keep unwanted visitors from crossing their boundary. The shape of Elhaz has at least three more protective interpretations.

First, Elhaz resembles the trunk and branches of a tree, offering shelter to protect all those in its scope. Elhaz is associated with the world tree Yggdrasil and therefore with horizontal travel between worlds throughout Yggdrasil's branches. Whereas Eihwaz governs travel to the upper or lower worlds, Elhaz governs travel to parallel worlds such as faerie-land, the ghost plane, and beyond the veil. Many entrances to faerie-land are said to be doors or gateways in or between trees. I also associate Elhaz with the family tree and the protection of my ancestors, both in the sense that their strength carried me here and carries me forward and that they watch and encourage me from the other side. Elhaz merkstave brings to mind the roots of a tree rather than its branches, in which case you are reminded that one of the best ways to protect and care for yourself is to stay rooted and firmly grounded in material reality, sometimes by staying put.

Second, the shape of Elhaz echoes the shape of a hand splayed in the universal sign for stop, which is seen in the Hamsa, which is said to protect against the evil eye. In this sense, it is a rune of self-defense, boundaries, and your ability to protect yourself with the strength of your own will.

Third, Elhaz resembles the long neck and splayed wings of a swan in flight, which is a symbol of the Valkyries, mythical female guardians of soldiers in battle. It is a rune of protection.

Elhaz may show up to remind you of all the protections that are already in place to keep you safe, as well as protective measures for which you are responsible. Other times, Elhaz appears to command you to stop because you're approaching a boundary. Merkstave, Elhaz may indicate that the situation is not safe or additional protection is necessary, or it may be a prompt to reconnect with your roots. Depending on the situation and context, Elhaz inverted may also mean it is safe to drop your shields, or that you have to do so for the matter to progress.

Practical Magic

Elhaz is ideally suited to protective talismans, especially for travelers (but suitable for anyone). Inscribe it onto your palms to empower your personal defenses and boundary-setting abilities, which is especially useful when defending yourself against unwelcome spirits. Write Elhaz on the backs of family photos or carve it into a frame of a family portrait to invoke the protective blessings of your ancestors. Display Elhaz on or above your door to protect the home. It may be especially wise to wear or carry Elhaz when working with spirits on the other side.

ANCESTRAL PROTECTION

Get in touch with your ancestors. They have passed on, but they can still protect you from beyond the veil. Start by learning something about them. Take a DNA test, research your genealogy, or dig through old photos and start asking questions. Call your oldest living relative and ask them to tell you something about your family's past that you didn't know. If you don't have any living ancestors, research your cultural history through books, the Internet, or public records. Find something in your ancestral past to connect to, and explore that connection through art, journaling, meditation, or divination.

Learning about the literal and metaphorical battles your ancestors fought so you could have the privilege of being alive today will help you understand that you could not have made it this far without generations of people fighting to propagate and protect your bloodline. The protective power of thousands of generations of mothers is no joke. Tune in to it, do what you need to anchor your knowledge of that protection in reality, and invoke Elhaz whenever you need to call upon that protective power.

SOWILO

Pronunciation: SO-wee-lo

Also Known As: Sowilo, Sol, Sig

Sound: S as in "sun"

Translation: Sun

Keywords: Sun, success, strength, illumination, clarity, guidance

MODERN MEANINGS

Sowilo is the rune of the sun. The sun provides illumination to help you see clearly and guide you on your journey. It burns through clouds and fog, bringing light and clarity. Depending on the context, Sowilo may indicate that certain things will soon come to light, or that your perception is already clear and unclouded. Just as the warmth of the sun overpowers the cold of winter and thaws the frozen earth, Sowilo represents the victory of light over darkness. It is a rune of success and may augur warmer, brighter, happier days ahead. Sowilo represents the life force and all other forms of solar energy and power.

Sowilo resembles a bolt of lightning, another sort of sky-fire, but although the sun can be treacherous in its own right, lightning gets all the credit for being dynamic and dangerous. As lightning is the bridge between heaven and earth, Sowilo governs contact between humans and the divine, and the transfer of the divine spark.

When Sowilo appears in a future position, it may herald the coming of the light: clarity and illumination, warmer and brighter days, or the victory of light and life over darkness and death. In the present, it may indicate that your position already allows you to see the situation clearly and things are indeed as they seem. Sowilo cannot appear merkstave, but in a negative context, it may be inverted, weakened, or perverted. Its inverse and weakened meanings include a lack of clarity, literal or metaphorical darkness, a shortage of vitamin D, or poor mental or physical health. Its perverse meanings include the usual symptoms of too much sun (sunburn, dehydration) and metaphorical variations on that theme (too much information, excess energy, blinding brightness). The worst perversion is the misrepresentation of personal hate-based agendas masquerading as hope for a brighter future, such as Walter Heck's appropriation of this rune for the Schutzstaffel insignia.

Practical Magic

Two Sowilo runes overlaid perpendicular to each other create a solar wheel, an ancient symbol of the sacred and benevolent power of the sun. Be careful about using this symbol in public because it is still often misused as a hate symbol. You can use the clockwise solar wheel to draw in solar qi, and the counterclockwise version to discharge it. As an alternative to this better-known but politically charged symbol, you can create a wheel-of-four Sowilo rune such that the bases meet at the center. Sowilo also makes a good talisman for success in tests, interviews, and presentations.

SUN TEA

Take advantage of the next sunny day to make a bottle of supercharged Sowilo sun tea.

1. Fill a clear glass bottle with clean spring water and the tea or herbs you want to infuse.

   • Sun tea brews weaker than tea made with boiling water, so use two to three times the tea you would normally.

   • For a single serving, I use three tea bags, or 15 grams, of tea, but fine-tune by feel.

   • Black tea (aka red tea or *hong cha*) makes a great sun tea.

   • St. John's Wort and yellow chrysanthemum are great herbal choices for caffeine-free solar infusions.

2. In red, mark Sowilo one or more times on the outside of the bottle.

3. Place the bottle outdoors in full sun and let steep a full 24 hours.

4. The next day, strain out the solids and enjoy.

   For the most authentic bottled sunlight experience, imbibe immediately outdoors. As you drink it, soak up some sunlight and meditate on the mysteries of Sowilo.

CHAPTER

8

THE THIRD ÆTT

The third and final ætt is Tyr's Ætt. Tyr is a god of war, justice, law, and order, and the runes in his ætt govern the ins and outs of human society and social structures. Tiwaz and Berkana offer new perspective on the divine masculine and feminine, acting as mother and father at the head of this ætt. They are followed by Ehwaz and Mannaz, which between them govern partnership, personal identity, self-reliance, friendship, and humanity. Laguz and Ingwaz represent the feminine and masculine fertilizing principles in the context of agriculture. Dagaz reconciles opposite complementary principles and reinforces the inevitability of change. In the final position, Othala reinforces the boundary *between* chaos and order, society and the great beyond. It is a rune of homecoming, return, and completion.

You may have noticed that many runes are *so* complex in their meanings that it seems a wonder that we can derive any specific meaning through divination. Remember, the runes do not do the thinking for you. They present you with new perspectives and the seeds of ideas to stimulate your own thinking. Each rune is nuanced, representing more than its keywords, and you must think intuitively and analytically about its significance and the best way to move forward. The meanings in this guidebook are intended to stimulate your intuition, creativity, and curiosity; they are not intended as a universal answer key. Good luck, and *reyn til runa*!

TIWAZ

Pronunciation: TEE-wahz

Also Known As: Teiwaz, Tyr, Tir, Ti

Sound: T as in "tea"

Translation: The god Tyr

Keywords: Justice, truth, righteousness, god, Tyr, law, trial by combat, kings/leaders/generals, the way, North Star, polestar, guidance, order, divine masculine, Irminsul

MODERN MEANINGS

Tiwaz is often called the victory rune. It is the rune of Tyr, the Norse god of justice and war who sacrificed one of his hands in the course of betraying and binding Fenrir, a fearsome wolf and child of Loki who was prophesied to bring great trouble to the Æsir. Tyr's betrayal of Fenrir was in service of the protection of Ásgarðr and the prevention of Ragnarök (the end of the world). Sometimes we have to commit a small injustice to prevent a larger one. Tiwaz reminds you that the compromises you make must serve your highest good and deepest core values. Tiwaz often appears as a reminder of your code of ethics and highest transcendent value, or guiding star. Tiwaz and Tyr are associated with the polestar (aka the North Star, Polaris), so Tiwaz is a rune of navigation and guidance. Additionally, Tiwaz represents the Irminsul, the pillar that was thought to uphold the order of the cosmos.

In a reading, Tiwaz may indicate that what it refers to is true, right, just, or fair. It may also be a call to speak, seek, or examine the truth, or to return to your center or true calling. Tiwaz commands you to determine what is true and important and act accordingly. Merkstave, it may indicate falsehood, deceit, treachery, injustice, dishonesty, or a lack of ethics or core values.

Practical Magic

Invoke Tiwaz in matters of justice and law, but only if you truly believe yourself to be in the right. Tiwaz's influence is in favor of the righteous and the honorable. If truth and justice are on your side, invoking Tiwaz may make fate your ally as well.

You can use Tiwaz to strengthen positive masculine qi, pierce through falsehood and deceit, empower someone with the courage to tell the truth, and help you rise above injustice and oppression.

VICTORY RUNES

In the Sigdrifumal (part of the Poetic Edda), the hero is advised that if he seeks victory, he should carve victory runes upon the hilt and blade of his sword and invoke Tyr twice. It is unclear whether the Tyr to be invoked is the god or the rune, but either way, it is the cosmic ordering force of justice and righteousness in the world. Such victory runes have been found carved onto weapons of war, typically in the form of multiple iterations of Tiwaz stacked into a single formation.

You probably don't use a sword in your day-to-day life, but what do you fight your battles with? Inscribe Tiwaz runes on your weapon of choice. Rehearsing for a battle of the bands? It can't hurt to add a line of victory runes down your drumsticks or the neck of your guitar. Need to hit that word count on a report? Slap some victory runes on your keyboard. Need to pass that test you've been studying for? Carve victory runes into your wooden pencil. Whatever you do, don't forget to charge them, and may the best runester win!

BERKANA

Pronunciation: BEAR-ka-nah

Also Known As: Berkanan, Beorc, Bjarkan

Sound: B as in "breathe"

Translation: Birch tree

Keywords: Birth, birch, earth mother, goddess, mother, womb, nourish, medicine, chaga, healing, life, verdant, fertile, divine feminine

MODERN MEANINGS

Berkana encompasses the birth and death mysteries governed by the divine feminine. It can be connected with Jörð (Earth goddess and mother of Thor), Frigg (Mother goddess and queen of Ásgarðr), Hela (Death goddess and lady of the grave), and the various triple goddesses of life, death, and rebirth. Whereas Perthro represents the literal womb and grave from whence life comes and to which it shall return, Berkana represents the mothering force that bestows life at the beginning and accepts our dead bodies at the end. It can be seen pictographically as the nurturing breasts of the earth mother, and is primarily a rune of life, loving care, shelter, nourishment, good health, and the feminine mysteries, including the mysteries of the blood.

Literally, it may indicate a woman, especially a mother, or in some instances a child. Berkana may also come up around menstruation, pregnancy, and motherhood. Motherhood is not always literal, however—the nurturing of any person or project applies here. On a similar note, it may appear with the purpose of calling you closer to Mother Earth. Merkstave Berkana may signal overattachment and codependence, or a lack of health or positive self-care habits. Often, Berkana merkstave indicates something or someone is not in good health or receiving proper care. It may also indicate a perversion of the nurturing principle whereby one gives of oneself in excess, which is unsustainable.

Practical Magic

You can invoke Berkana to support menstruation, pregnancy, lactation, motherhood, and menopause. Use henna, woad, beet juice, or washable marker to apply it to your womb or breasts to help ease cramping and soreness, or to your lower back for hormonal back pain. More generally, you can apply Berkana to support healing of any kind. Write it on bandages, carve it into root vegetables before cooking and eating them, paint it on casts and splints, and inscribe it onto the packaging of supplements and medications. You may want to apply Berkana to your favorite mug so you can imbibe its blessings on a daily basis.

BERKANA BREW

Where birch trees grow, you will often find chaga, a cold-climate parasitic fungus sometimes known as King of the Mushrooms. Chaga supports physical health and immune function in a number of ways, and contains compounds with antioxidant, anti-inflammatory, and anticarcinogenic properties. You can take it internally as a tea or tincture and apply it topically in the form of an oil or salve.

If you require a higher dose of Berkana vibes and are ready to level up your self-care routine, make some space in your home for a slow cooker where you can always have chaga brewing. Purchase lumps of chaga and wrap approximately 1 ounce in cheesecloth and kitchen twine or place it in a muslin bag. Fill the slow cooker with clean spring water, add the chaga, and leave it to simmer overnight. When you first brew it, the chaga broth should be rich and dark and taste earthy. You may like it plain or with honey and cinnamon, or you can mask the flavor but keep the benefits by using it to brew your favorite tea or pour-over coffee. Alternatively, you can chill batches of chaga and enjoy it plain or mixed with cold brew coffee. Each time you take from your chaga pot, add more water and let it continue brewing. After a few weeks, the liquid will become very diluted. At this point, replace your chaga chunks and use the old ones in a foot soak, give them to the garden, or dry them out and use them to make a tincture.

EHWAZ

Pronunciation: EH-wahz

Also Known As: Eoh, Eh

Sound: E as in "ballet"

Translation: Horse

Keywords: Harmony, divine twins, horse, partnership, synergy, intimacy

MODERN MEANINGS

The literal meaning of Ehwaz is "horse." The partnership between a horse and its rider is a sacred and ineffable bond. They depend on and care for each other in their own ways. Lovers may have a similar bond, and in this sense, Ehwaz is a rune of dynamic partnership. It is associated with the archetype of the lovers and interpersonal harmony. Ehwaz governs partnerships and relationships of all kinds, and it represents and encourages collaboration and cooperation. It is also associated with the divine twins, Freyr and Freyja (lord and lady of the Vanir), and the constellation Gemini.

We cannot mention horses in Norse mythology without discussing Sleipnir, Óðinn's eight-legged steed (and another child of Loki). Sleipnir, which basically translates to "Slippy," serves the special purpose of carrying Óðinn into other worlds through inner journeys, which was seen as an important role of horses in the northern spiritual tradition. Yggdrasil, the name of the world tree, means "Yggr's steed" (Yggr is one of the many names of Óðinn). In his runic initiation, Óðinn "rides" the tree. On his other journeys, he rides Sleipnir, and together they "slip" through the doors between worlds. Thus, Ehwaz is also a rune of trancework, inner journeys, the etheric body used for such journeys, travel, and transportation. It can also refer to spirit guides who assist you during your inner journeys as well as your day-to-day waking life. Ehwaz reminds you that you are not alone, and that you can lean on others as they may need to lean on you. Pictographically, you can see the rune as two horse heads facing each other and meeting in the middle, two people holding hands, or the legs and body of a standing horse, ready to bear a rider.

In a reading, Ehwaz can refer to a partner or relationship, or to harmony, synergy, or the need for cooperation. It can also refer to travel, transportation, and vehicles—anything that helps you move, literally or metaphorically, from point A to point B. Inverted, it can indicate discord, conflict, an imbalanced partnership, codependence, or a resistance to giving or receiving support. Ehwaz merkstave can also indicate entrapment, as someone who lacks social support or transportation might feel.

Practical Magic

Call upon Ehwaz to encourage healthy, loving relationships and strengthen existing ones, or to support healing toxic or codependent relationship patterns. In relationship magic, Ehwaz mixes well with Gebo; in community-building, pair it with Wunjo.

Wear or carry Ehwaz during inner journeys to slip more easily into a trance state and support interplanar travel. If you have physical representations of any of your spirit guides, you can mark them with this rune to reinforce your bond, such as on the back of a photo or the feet of an animal figurine. For the ultimate trancework talisman, create a bindrune of Ehwaz, Eihwaz, and Elhaz.

LOVE LETTERS

How is the bond represented by Ehwaz manifested in your life? Do you have a musical instrument, vehicle, pet, romantic partner, best friend, twin, or spirit guide with whom you have an ineffable mutual bond? If so, write them a love letter, or send one to an ideal partner. Thank them for their support, tell them how much you appreciate them, and commit to support them, too. When you are done, sign Ehwaz near your name and charge it (after all, this rune is a sort of love letter in itself). Afterward, if you wrote to an actual person, give them the letter. If you wrote to someone or something else, you can read it, burn it, or bury it to ritually give it to them. If you wrote to someone you're still manifesting, burn the letter to send it off and let the universe know what sort of partnership you're ready for, or include it in the Jera spell from chapter 7.

MANNAZ

Pronunciation: MAH-nahz

Also Known As: Mann, Maðr

Sound: M as in "mirror"

Translation: Man, human, mankind

Keywords: Humanity, man, people, mirror/reflection, relationships, people, companionship, social, fallibility of mankind

MODERN MEANINGS

Mannaz means "man," as in "humankind," as opposed to gods, giants, and other beings. People are curious, creative, social, and extremely fallible beings. The old rune poems make clear their impression of humans: we're pretty great, even better together, but you can't *really* depend on any of us, and we all die in the end. Like every other rune, Mannaz has its positives and negatives, just as we humans have our good days and our bad ones. Sometimes we're reminded of just how much we need human interaction; other times, we realize we can only truly depend on ourselves.

Pictographically, Mannaz can be seen as two people facing each other, or Wunjo mirrored (double joy). Thus, Mannaz represents the common thread of humanity found within each of us as well as the beauty and necessity of our individual differences and the joy we can find in seeing eye to eye with each other. In a reading, Mannaz may refer to relationships and social life, your self-concept and strength of identity, or the virtues of fidelity and self-reliance. Sometimes it shows up to remind you to call a friend or to schedule social activities or time for yourself. Mannaz can also serve as a reminder of all we have in common—a relentless desire to exist and explore, a need for meaning, a need for each other, the inability to meet our own unrealistic standards and those of others, and a weakness for short-term pleasures. Merkstave, Mannaz may indicate poor mental health, a weakened sense of self, an unreliable social network, or lack of a social life. Mannaz may also appear merkstave to draw attention to the weaknesses and fallibility of humanity as they apply to the matter at hand.

Practical Magic

Call upon Mannaz to aid with self-actualization and strengthening personality and identity. Mannaz can also support empathy, communication, self-awareness, social awareness, and the pursuit of human rights.

Invoke the Mannaz rune in meeting spaces before gatherings to encourage an affable atmosphere and set the space energetically. Mannaz can be especially helpful for making a good impression during interviews and whenever you meet someone new. To make the most of this, wear or carry it on your person when heading to job interviews, first dates, cocktail hours, or other networking events. You can also call upon Mannaz to assist with developing personal character and seeing and appreciating another person for who they truly are.

MAN IN THE MIRROR

To relieve stress from overly high expectations of yourself, temporarily inscribe Mannaz in the center of your forehead and over your heart chakra. Get in front of a mirror, take yourself in, and meditate on Mannaz and the nature of humanity. Remind yourself that you are only human and you are doing the best you can, and breathe deeply. Repeat the following: *"Mannaz, Mannaz, Mannaz. I am only human. Mannaz, Mannaz, Mannaz. I am mighty human."* Really look at the miracle that is your face, your body, your hands. Take a moment to appreciate your eyes, ears, mouth, neck, spine, hips, legs, and feet and all they do. Know that your best is good enough. Breathe in the awe of the miracle of your existence, acknowledge the weaknesses of your material body, express gratitude to your human vessel, and enjoy it while you can.

LAGUZ

Pronunciation: LAH-gooz

Also Known As: Laukaz, Lagu, Lögr

Sound: L as in "leak"

Translation: Leek or lake

Keywords: Life force, water, lake, leek, leak, flood, flow, spring, shoots and sprouts, ocean, sea, waterfall, fountain, moon, mead

MODERN MEANINGS

Laguz is water, the source of all life. No known life can go on without it, all known life came from it, and it makes up most of your body, yet it remains both deadly and mysterious. At the beginning of the Norse creation story, fire and ice came together and created the first life-forms as the ice was melted. Miðgarðr was said to have been brought up from out of the sea, and many people believe Atlantis was lost to it. After death, the ancient Norse were often buried in boat-shaped graves (or with actual boats) to carry them safely to the afterlife.

Three wells or springs are featured in Norse mythology and can be associated with Laguz: Urðarbrunnr, the Well of Urðr or Well of Wyrd, from whence came the runes and from which the Norns water Yggdrasil; Mímisbrunnr, Mímir's well of wisdom and memory, where Óðinnn's eye is hidden; and Hvergelmir, or "Roaring Cauldron," a bubbling spring in Niflheimr from whence all other waters are said to rise and which is home to a dragon and innumerable snakes. Each has something to hide, but is also a source of wisdom and the life force. Laguz literally means "lake," "water," or "waterfall," but by way of Norse wordplay can also mean "leek," a fertility symbol that embodies the principles of wellness, resilience, and renewal. Laguz is that which bubbles up and bursts forth, like water from an underground spring or leaks from moist green earth.

Sowilo and the sun are associated with Óðinn's remaining eye (clear sight), and Laguz and the moon are associated with the eye Óðinn sacrificed to Mímisbrunnr (inner vision or memory). Tides, reflections, and hidden dark sides are all things water shares with the moon, and one could think of Laguz as a lunar rune. With its connection to the moon and being a rune of water and life, Laguz is also a rune of the blood mysteries. It is the water of the womb from which we originate, and the blood that runs through our veins. Laguz also governs the tides of moods, the ebb and flow of emotions.

In a reading, Laguz can refer to literal water and may appear as a call to spend time near water, take a cleansing shower or relaxing bath, or drink water (hydrate or diedrate). It can also refer to emotions and matters of the heart (or hormones), memories, or something new coming up. Laguz is generally a positive rune, especially in matters of health, but it has a characteristic fluidity. It is less about fortitude and power than resilience and flexibility.

Laguz can refer to the moon, menstruation and women's health, or a month. Depending on context, it may indicate that something is coming up, flowing, growing, fluid, or flooded. An excess of Laguz is flood, fickleness, or emotional overflow. A perversion of Laguz is oblivion, mania, mold, hypersensuality, inconstancy, alcoholism, or leakage. The absence of Laguz is drought, dryness, brittleness, dehydration, death, disease, blockage, inflexibility, inactivity, or forgetfulness. Laguz merkstave may indicate any of these.

Practical Magic

Laguz is central to the ancient rune formula ALU (ᚨᛚᚢ), which is used to give life to magical items and awaken runic inscriptions. It is the gift of lifeblood that Loðurr gives Ask and Embla. Laguz can be invoked as a rune of cleansing, especially emotionally, spiritually, and energetically. Inscribe it on your water bottle to reinforce the hydrating, cleansing, and healing power of the water you drink, and to support longevity. You can also use it to support menstruation, arousal, and healing.

MAGICAL BATHING

Magical baths support healing and renewal. You want to soak your clean body in clean water, so shower first. A bath serves as the cauldron of rebirth, the symbolic womb. You emerge from it renewed and perhaps transformed. While you are in the bath, you are in the stage between caterpillar and butterfly. You are in the goo phase, and you can remake yourself in the image of your highest self. Add various elements to the bath to augment its magical and physical functions.

It is a good idea to start with plain Epsom salts, as the magnesium in the salts will soothe the muscles and relax the mind. Then add herbs and flowers, oils, and crystals. Some of my favorite combinations include lavender and amethyst, to encourage relaxation and inner vision; rose and rose quartz, to encourage love and sensuality; chamomile, oats, and coconut milk, to calm the mind and soothe the skin; and green tea and citrine, for a clear mind and a bright outlook. Before you enter the bath, activate the Laguz rune on the surface of the water, and feel its renewing light wash over you as you enter the water. Stay in as long as necessary to emerge renewed.

INGWAZ

Pronunciation: ING-wahz

Also Known As: Ing, Inguz

Sound: NG as in "king"

Translation: The god Freyr (aka Ing/Yngvi)

Keywords: Seed, fertility, stored potential, gestation, new beginnings, kings, masculine fertility, new projects, ideas, chrysalis

MODERN MEANINGS

Ingwaz is the rune of the god Ing, an aspect of Freyr. It is a rune of masculine fertility, agriculture, and kings. Ingwaz is the seed of potential that grows within the womb. It is the principle of fertilization, gestation, ripening, and internal transformation. If Laguz is the primordial water from which life emerges, Ingwaz is the seed and the beginning of life that enters into that water (the wet earth or the womb). This parallels an ancient belief that the fortune of a kingdom depended on the divine favor, right behavior, and virility of the king. If the kingdom was suffering or the king was infertile, he had a duty to vacate the position.

When Ingwaz appears in a reading, it may indicate a state of fertility or slow ripening (gestation) regarding the subject at hand. It is a good time to plant (begin projects) but not yet time to harvest (reap the rewards). Ingwaz can refer to boys and children, young or virile men, conception, lineage, productivity, an investment, potential, or new beginnings. Ingwaz cannot appear merkstave, but in a negative position may indicate infertility, barrenness, emptiness, or failure.

Practical Magic

Ingwaz can be invoked to aid fertilization and germination when planting, and complements Fehu and Jera nicely in the garden. You can also call upon it to support male virility and encourage conception. Afterward, you can place it on the expecting mother's womb to magically support healthy fetal development.

MAGICAL BATTERIES

A magical battery is anything that is magically charged for later use in a magical working. Magical batteries are useful for a number of reasons. It may not be the right time to harvest the subtle energies you need for a working when you need them, or you may not *have* time. Perhaps an energetically potent event is coming to pass, and you have no particular need of it at that time but want to use it later. Water and crystals work well as magical batteries, and runes can shape and flavor the qi you raise and store.

For a basic magical battery charged with whatever intention you like for later activation, start with a glass bottle or mason jar. Fill it with good spring water, and drop a small clear quartz crystal in the bottom. On the lid or on the vessel itself, inscribe Ingwaz. Add other runes *inside* Ingwaz to form and flavor your intention. Then, charge the runes as directed in chapter 3. When this is done, you can raise or capture magical energy (qi) by meditating, chanting, singing, dancing, creating friction, playing an instrument, or using another method. You can also use the battery to capture moonlight, sunlight, eclipse light, starlight (on a dark moon with a clear sky), or firelight. When you want to use it, simply include some or all of the water in your magical working.

DAGAZ

Pronunciation: DAH-gahz

Also Known As: Dæg

Sound: D as in "door" or ð (voiced "th") as in "father"

Translation: Day

Keywords: Day, new day, dawn, door, dusk, in-between, gateway, paradox, liminal, veil, threshold, breakthrough, transformation, point of no return

MODERN MEANINGS

The most straightforward way to interpret Dagaz is literally: It is the day, the warm golden domain of the sun. But Dagaz is not merely daytime—it is the dawning of a new day, the return of the light, the point of transition from darkness to light. This rune is associated specifically with the winter solstice, but it's appropriate for any transition: dawn, dusk, eclipses, rites of passage, and the moments of birth and death. Dagaz is also associated with liminal spaces, such as thresholds, doorways, doors, gates, the veil, and the horizon. Pictographically, it resembles a double door or gateway. In a question of either/or, Dagaz almost always means "yes, and . . ." It is an optimistic rune that denies the mutual exclusivity of opposite principles and perspectives. Its shape also resembles the lemniscate, the sign of infinity.

Nearly every rune has at least two complementary and seemingly paradoxical aspects, and that is not Dagaz's claim to uniqueness. Dagaz does not so much *have* two paradoxical meanings as its meaning *is* paradox. It is the fulcrum, the in-between, and the pattern of simultaneous duality. It is the necessity that everything has its opposite and complement. It is the reality that two conflicting perspectives can both be true, that light has no meaning without darkness, that life has no meaning without death.

Dagaz is a rune of transformation and breakthrough, and may indicate that you are on the edge of a breakthrough in understanding, approaching a climax of tension, or experiencing some sort of transformation or transition (cue Lady Gaga's "The Edge of Glory"). These times can feel quite chaotic, but that is the nature of change.

In a reading, Dagaz may herald brighter days ahead or some sort of turning point. It is certain that a new day *will* come. The darkest moments are often just before the dawn, so stick it out. Dagaz may also appear as a call to make the most of the days you are given. While Dagaz is an optimistic rune, it reminds us that the glass is *definitely* half-full *and* half-empty. Dagaz cannot appear merkstave, and it can't really have a negative context because it is by nature both sides of the story.

Practical Magic

You can invoke Dagaz to aid in finding suitable compromises and mutually agreeable outcomes. It supports transformational magic, and it can be combined with other runes according to the nature of the transformation. Wear or carry Dagaz to ease transitions and support rites of passage.

DRAWING DOORS

With caution and careful consideration, you can open doors into alternate realms of perception by drawing Dagaz in the air. It is easiest to pass through the doors when they are drawn in some sort of natural portal, like a doorway, an archway, or between two trees. Draw it with your finger or wand while intoning its name. When you can perceive the glowing door-rune with your subtle senses, peer through (vibe check it). If it feels good, walk on through. You may feel as though your perception has been temporarily heightened and you might notice things for the first time. Record and reflect on your thoughts and observations. A quick word of caution to would-be travelers: Make sure you remember where you came from and where you want to end up.

OTHALA

Pronunciation: OH-tha-lah

Also Known As: Othalan, Ethel, Oðal

Sound: O as in "home"

Translation: Heritage, estate

Keywords: Inheritance, family, ancestry, inner circle, enclosure, intimacy, estate, home, homeland, heritage, society, culture

MODERN MEANINGS

As you arrive at the final rune of the futhark, with the sun of a new day coming over the hill, you have returned home at last. Othala is home, family, the estate, and all that you receive from your ancestors. Othala is that which is inherited and cannot be transferred, such as physical characteristics, genetic predispositions, genetic memory, family titles, culture, and even blessings, curses, special talents, and behavioral patterns that are passed down through generations. Othala is also the rune of the estate and the home or homeland. The shape of the rune creates an enclosure, which is one of its meanings: Othala is the boundary that separates the familiar from the unfamiliar. Among modern Heathens, the words *innangarðr* and *útangarðr* are used to distinguish between the two, although this usage can be traced back only to the late 20th century. *Garðr* refers to an enclosure, such as a fence or wall. That which is innangarðr is indoors or within the enclosure, and that which is útangarðr is outdoors or beyond the enclosure. The innangarðr is safe, familiar, and orderly ("Everything the light touches is our kingdom"); the útangarðr is unfamiliar, and often dangerous ("What about that shadowy place way out there?"). Othala asks us to examine our personal innangarðr and útangarðr and reminds us that all the water in the world cannot sink a boat it cannot penetrate.

Othala can also refer to family in general or to specific family members, especially direct ancestors and descendants. It can also refer to the home, sacred space, and your personal bubble, society, or social group.

It may appear as a reminder to give thanks for the body and blood you have inherited. In a reading, Othala may appear to remind you of what your parents and more distant ancestors have handed down, including mannerisms, family wisdom, intergenerational trauma, and even skills or recipes. Othala can also indicate something coming full circle, back to the beginning, returning to home base. The return home can be seen to take place on the same level of the spiral or at the same position on a new level of the spiral. In other words, you can go home to the place you were born and raised, or you can go home to heaven. Either way, homecoming is a joyous thing.

Merkstave, Othala can indicate a weak boundary between innangarðr and útangarðr and a dissolution of order. It may indicate a lack of familial ties or ancestral connection, or a rejection of heritage or inheritance. In other words, Othala merkstave may be a rune of rebellion, chaos, and upheaval, as it symbolizes the dominance of the útangarðr and the rejection of the innangarðr. Othala is sometimes perverted as a symbol of racial purity, so Othala merkstave may also indicate racism or other aggressively exclusionary tactics and philosophies.

Practical Magic

Use Othala to mark the boundaries of your home, property, safe spaces, and sacred enclosures to magically reinforce and secure them. This rune is especially well suited to hanging over doors that connect the inside and outside. Inscribe, wear, or carry Othala on your person to connect more deeply and come to terms with your family, ancestry, and cultural heritage. Some people think taking pride in one's heritage means believing that others are inferior, but Othala is not about racial purity. It's about the generations that have conspired to bring each of us here today and continue to protect us today.

HOUSE BLESSING

House blessings are easy to do and can go a long way toward setting good vibes in a home. This is the basic process, which you can embellish according to your needs.

The first step is a simple cleansing. Move through every part of the home and cleanse it energetically by doing one or more of the following: ring a bell or chime, play a singing bowl, sweep, burn herbs or incense (like rosemary, juniper, or copal), spritz a magical cleansing spray, or sprinkle salt water. It helps to do some physical tidying first.

After cleansing, bless the house by once again walking throughout the living space and doing one or more of the following: burn herbs, spices, or incense (sage to sanctify, mint for prosperity, cinnamon for warmth); mop with essential oils; sing or play music. Speak to the house of all the blessings you wish for it and call the blessings in out loud ("*May this house . . .*," "*May all who enter here . . .*," "*May all who live here . . .*"). Envision each blessing as you speak it. Open the windows if you can and let in as much light as possible.

When you have finished your rounds, visit the external doors and charge Othala on each of them to seal the blessings inside the home and solidify the spiritual boundary around it.

House blessings go hand in hand with housewarmings. When you are finished, have some friends over to help rub in all the good vibes so they stick around as long as possible. House cleansings and blessings can be performed as needed, though once or twice a year is typically sufficient.

RESOURCES

The Big Book of Runes and Rune Magic: How to Interpret Runes, Rune Lore, and the Art of Runecasting by Edred Thorsson

This book includes the best overview of runic history and the runic revival I have found, alongside information on Norse cosmology, mythology, and other resources. This book also covers Thorsson's take on runic divination, which his more famous title *Futhark* does not.

The Nine Doors of Miðgarðr: A Curriculum of Rune-work by Edred Thorsson

This text is the core curriculum for associates and learners of the Rune Gild. The book comes with a required reading list of its own, for those who are seriously interested in pursuing runic wisdom and attaining membership in the Rune Gild, an organization founded in 1979 for the purpose of raising future generations of rune masters. More information can be found at Rune-Gild.org.

Runes: The Icelandic Book of Futhark by Teresa Drofn Freysdottir Njardvik

This beautifully designed book provides bold graphics and brief prose interpretations of all the runes in the Elder Futhark, the Younger Futhark, and the Icelandic Futhark. It also includes relevant translations of the rune poems with each rune. It falls somewhere between a solid reference and an art piece.

Taking Up the Runes: A Complete Guide to Using Runes in Spells, Rituals, Divination, and Magic by Diana L. Paxson

Paxson surveys much of the extant rune literature before giving her take on each rune. The runes are examined sequentially in pairs, which adds a welcome layer of depth to her interpretations. Paxson's original contributions include suggestions and rituals for solitary and group work.

And more . . .

There are so many great resources available today for learning about the runes and everything that comes with them that I wish I had known about when I was first learning. To spare you the trouble of separating some of the wheat from the chaff, I've put together a more comprehensive directory of my favorite books, websites, videos, podcasts, and other rune-related resources for your browsing pleasure, which I will keep updated. You can find this at VervainAndTheRoses.com/resources.

REFERENCES

Adams, Douglas. *The Hitchhiker's Guide to the Galaxy*. New York: Del Rey, 1995.

Arild Hauge's Runes. Accessed December 21, 2019. Arild-Hauge.com/eindex.htm.

Aswynn, Freya. *Northern Mysteries & Magick: Runes, Gods, and Feminine Powers.* 2nd ed. St. Paul, MN: Llewellyn, 2002.

Bellows, Henry Adams, trans. *The Poetic Edda*. Princeton, NJ: Princeton University Press, 1936.

Blum, Ralph. *The Book of Runes: A Handbook for the Use of an Ancient Oracle*. New York: St. Martin's Press, 1984.

Bray, Olive, trans. *The Elder or Poetic Edda, Commonly Known as Sæmund's Edda, Part I: The Mythological Poems*. Vol. 2. London, Printed for the Viking Club, 1908. Archive.org/details/elderorpoeticedd01brayuoft/mode/2up.

Chapman, Gary D. *The 5 Love Languages: The Secret to Love That Lasts*. Chicago: Northfield, 2014. Kindle.

Chauran, Alexandra. "Witch's Runes: A Simple Introduction to Rune Reading." *Llewellyn Journal*, November 14, 2016. Llewellyn.com/journal/article/2599.

Crawford, Jackson. "Innangard and Utangard: Two Non-Words in Old Norse." Video, 4:48, January 11, 2020. YouTube.com/watch?v=xsIZneUeZQw&.

Gronitz, Dan. "Meanings." The Rune Site. Accessed December 21, 2019. TheRuneSite.com/section/rune-meanings.

Hostetter, Aaron K., trans. "The Rune Poem." Old English Poetry Project. Last modified. October 19, 2017. AngloSaxonPoetry.camden.rutgers.edu/the-rune-poem.

Internet Sacred Text Archive. "Hovamol: The Ballad of the High One." Accessed December 18, 2019. Sacred-Texts.com/neu/poe/poe04.htm.

Kaldera, Raven. "The Futhorc Runes." Northern-Tradition Shamanism. Accessed December 21, 2019. NorthernShamanism.org/the-futhorc-runes.html.

Kardach, Jim. "Tech History: How Bluetooth Got Its Name." EE Times, March 5, 2008. EETimes.com/tech-history-how-bluetooth-got-its-name/#.

Mees, Bernard. "The Etymology of Rune." Beiträge zur Geschichte der deutschen Sprache und Literatur 136, no. 4 (2014). Academia.edu/34915027/The_etymology_of_rune.

Morgan, Thad. "How Did the Vikings Honor Their Dead?" History.com. Last modified November 28, 2018. History.com/news/how-did-the-vikings-honor-their-dead.

Njardvik, Teresa Drofn Freysdottir. *Runes: The Icelandic Book of Fuþark*. Reykjavík: Icelandic Magic Company, 2019.

Norse Mythology for Smart People. NorseMythology.org. Accessed December 20, 2020.

Paxson, Diana L. *Taking Up the Runes: A Complete Guide to Using Runes in Spells, Rituals, Divination, and Magic*. York Beach, ME: Weiser Books, 2005.

Short, William R. "Stories, Poems, and Literature from the Viking Age." Hurstwic. Accessed December 18, 2019. Hurstwic.org/history/articles/literature/text/literature.htm.

Spiesberger, Karl. *Runenmagie: Handbuch der Runenkunde*. Berlin: Richard Schikowski, 1954. Neuseddin.eu/pdf/Runenmagie.pdf.

Stephens, George. *Handbook of the Old-Northern Runic Monuments of Scandinavia and England*. London: Williams and Norgate, 1884. Archive.org/details/cu31924026355499/page/n118/mode/1up/search/kragehul.

Þorgeirsson, Haukur. "Rúnatal." *Old Norse for Beginners*. Accessed December 20, 2020. Notendur.hi.is/haukurth/norse/reader/runatal.html.

Thorsson, Edred. *The Big Book of Runes and Rune Magic: How to Interpret Runes, Rune Lore, and the Art of Runecasting*. Newburyport, MA: Weiser Books, 2018.

Thorsson, Edred. *Futhark: A Handbook of Rune Magic*. Newburyport, MA: Weiser Books, 2012.

Tolkien, J. R. R. *The Fellowship of the Ring*. London: George Allen & Unwin, Ltd., 1954.

Towrie, Sigurd. "Maeshowe's Runes—Viking Graffiti." Orkneyjar. Accessed December 18, 2019. Orkneyjar.com/history/maeshowe/maeshrunes.htm.

University of Richmond. "TACITUS *Germania*." Accessed December 18, 2019. FacultyStaff.Richmond.edu/~wstevens/history331texts/barbarians.html.

Ward, Christie. "Runes and Writing." Viking Answer Lady. Accessed December 21, 2019. VikingAnswerLady.com/callig.shtml.

Willis, Tony. *Discover Runes: Understanding and Using the Power of Runes*. New York: Sterling, 1993.

RUNE INDEX

INDEX

W

Web of Wyrd, 1, 32, 44
Well of Urðr, 3, 8
Wheel of the Year spread, 52–55
Wiligut, Karl Maria, 13
Wotanism, 13

Y

Yggdrasil, 3, 8
Younger Futhark runes, 5, 6

ACKNOWLEDGMENTS

I owe a huge debt to all the rune scholars and magicians of the past and present who have seen fit to publish their findings in print or online, especially those who continue to dedicate energy to rune research and education. Without their efforts, I never would have had access to what has become one of my most valuable tools for transformation and insight. To Edred Thorsson, Diana Paxson, and the dozen others in my bibliography and on my bookshelf (or in my bookmarks), thank you for paving the way for future generations to explore the magic of the runes.

I wanted to write this book for years before I was approached for this project, but because I was still learning, I felt I wasn't ready. I realize now that if we all waited to write about the runes until after we understood them completely, there would be no rune books. To Joe at Callisto Media thank you for reaching out and believing in me. It was your call that let me know I was ready. To my editor, Sean, thank you for trusting me with this opportunity and for your perennial patience as I found my way through the words.

There is no way I would have survived the past few months without the wholehearted support and cooperation of my wonderful husband, Shawn. He has taken on so much more than his fair share to help out while I've had my nose buried half in rune-stuff and half in psychology textbooks. Shawn, thank you for your love, patience, and understanding; for talking philosophy, religion, spirituality, and magic with me for the past seven years (and the next forever); for grilling fishes so delicious they break my hyperfocus; for doing so many of the dishes; and for all those lovely cups of coffee.

To my parents, thank you for encouraging my strange childhood interests and my creativity; for modeling the highest levels of productivity I've ever witnessed; and for being so incredibly, unimaginably patient and supportive as I continue to learn and grow. I am proud and grateful to be your daughter.

To my dear friends Abigail and Erica, thank you for always being ready and willing to talk about the runes and all the lessons they have to teach, and for showing up for me in every other possible way.

To my wonderful friend and housemate Ella, thank you for inspiring and encouraging my own magic to grow these past five years alongside yours.

To all my gods, guides, and guardians, thank you for protecting me and for helping me find the way forward through all shades of light and darkness.

And finally, to Óðinn . . . Rúnatýr, Galdraföðr, Alföðr, Vegtam, Grímnir, Oðr, God of Runes, and Master of Self. Words run dry. What words could I use to thank you that were not first inspired by you? My entire journey, far beyond just this book, has been made possible by the example of your sacrifice and your guidance, wisdom, love, inspiration, and gift of the word. Thank you, thank you, a thousand times thank you. I hope I have done your gifts justice, and that I may make good use of them all my days.

ABOUT THE AUTHOR

 **Vervain Helsdottir** is an eclectic Heathen witch, priestess, and author of the blog *Vervain and the Roses* (VervainAndTheRoses.com). She was called to the runes as a child and has been following the call ardently for the past seven years. More broadly, she has studied witchcraft and divination for the past 15 years and now works as a professional rune and tarot reader, among other things. A lifelong creatrix and hobby-philosopher obsessed with breaking down the barrier between the magical and the mundane, Vervain writes to bring thoughtful spirituality and everyday magic to an ever-accelerating world. She is a devotee of Óðinn, Hela, Freyja, and Guan Yin and a member of The Troth.

When she's not dancing naked in the moonlight or peering into the great beyond, Vervain can be found singer-songwriting, painting rainbow visions, studying psychology, pouring Gong Fu Cha, or—very occasionally—sleeping.

CPSIA information can be obtained
at www.ICGtesting.com
Printed in the USA
JSHW060031011122
32375JS00010B/102